Manopause

Bernard O'Shea is an Irish comedian and broadcaster. He co-hosted *Breakfast Republic* on 2FM for five years, wrote and starred in the hit RTÉ TV series *Bridget and Eamon* and was most recently seen on RTÉ's *Marty and Bernard: On the Road Again*. His first book, *My Wife is Married to a Feckin' Eejit*, was a bestseller.

Manopause

Bernard O'Shea

Gill Books

Gill Books
Hume Avenue
Park West
Dublin 12
www.gillbooks.ie

Gill Books is an imprint of M.H. Gill & Co.

© Bernard O'Shea 2020
978 07171 8968 7

Design and print origination by O'K Graphic Design, Dublin
Edited by Alison Walsh
Proofread by Esther Ní Dhonnacha
Printed by CPI Group (UK) Ltd, Croydon, CRO 4YY

This book is typeset in 13.5/17 pt Minion

The paper used in this book comes from the wood pulp of managed forests. For every tree felled, at least one tree is planted, thereby renewing natural resources.

A CIP catalogue record for this book is available from the British Library.

5 4 3 2 1

Contents

Introduction

I sat at the kitchen table in the house where I grew up in the middle of Ireland.

'Will you have a cup of tea?' my mother asked. Me and my mother are the only two people in the world who know how to make tea. Strong with a tiny drop of milk.

'I left the bag in for you,' she said, putting the cup on the counter. Leaving the teabag in the cup is one of those things that people either find disgusting or vital. I find it vital.

I still vividly remember my mother's 40th birthday. I was the only child left in the house. My three older sisters had all flown the nest and my mum, dad and our strong cups of tea were left alone to our odd devices in a typical country bungalow with a flat roof that always leaked.

'Life begins at 40, Mum,' I said to her at the kitchen table that morning before school. She thought it was hilarious. Now, I was 40, still sitting at that same table.

'Well, Bernard,' she said. 'As you told me that morning, life begins at 40.'

I laughed. 'I think I'm going through the manopause.'

'The what?'

I poured the tiniest amount of milk into my tea. 'The manopause ... the male menopause.'

She sat down and looked me sternly in the face. 'If you had any idea what the menopause was like, Bernard, believe me, *you wouldn't go through it. Sweating, hot flushes, no sleep – at times it feels like you are going mad.'*

She took a deep breath. 'You wouldn't survive 30 seconds of it. No man would survive it. Jesus, if ye did go through it, we'd never hear the end of it. And if you went through it, you'd hospitalise yourself. What makes you say that?'

I looked at my tea sheepishly. 'Erm … I'm writing a book about it.'

She sighed. 'Bernard, you really are a fecking eejit.'

I turned 40 on 24 March 2019.

For my birthday, my wife Lorna gave me the greatest present I've ever received: five free days to do whatever I wanted. She was taking the kids to her parents down the country and I could have the house to myself. For the first time in six years, I had no responsibilities. She instructed me to 'live like you're in your twenties again and if you do something stupid, I don't want to know about it'.

I didn't do anything remotely stupid. In fact, I'm embarrassed by my efforts. I lived very much like a man about to turn 40.

Those five days set in train an emotional rollercoaster as I contemplated my existence, got drunk on three pints of Guinness and made a fool of myself pretending to be a man half my age.

Over the next year, I would also attempt to eat soil, dislocate my kneecap for the umpteenth time and be embarrassing in front of a Millennial.

What follows is a true and honest record – more or less (my wife, Lorna, would say less because she knows I'm a liar) – of my year. I had all kinds of plans that never quite came to be, but I learned a lot about myself in this year of living not-so-dangerously. I learned that I take the easy way out, don't finish things I start, and have a tendency to exaggerate. It ended in me having to face facts and make real, lasting changes in my life, as well as finding God, then losing him again.

This is a record of the heroic struggle of my manopause.

PART ONE

My Birthday Vows

was totally floored by Lorna's present. At first, I was all 'Oh I'm going to miss you and the kids so much' and 'I want to celebrate with you guys,' but inside I was doing backflips. I met Lorna when I was twenty-eight and she was twenty-three. We were married two years later. Within the blink of an eye we had three kids under six – Olivia, Tadhg and Seán – and a mortgage. She has built up catchphrases to describe me over the last ten years and her most frequent one is 'You just want to live in a one-bed apartment in town and play your guitar and watch football.' I couldn't deny it. Living with small kids is so much harder than I'd thought. They don't sleep, they demand things constantly and they put yogurt EVERYWHERE. I love them to bits, but a five-day break was possibly the most amazing thing that had ever happened to me. I would be on my own for the first time in seven years.

As the car pulled out of the driveway, the kids were ecstatically waving goodbye.

They knew a Mayan-style celebration of chocolate would greet them in Granny and Grandad's, so they were not in the least upset to say goodbye to their father. Lorna shouted, 'Enjoy the last few days of your thirties, bachelor boy.'

Their father has grown considerably in size since he was a bachelor. Just ten years ago, before I met their mother, I was twelve-and-a-half stone. As I waved them off, I stood in the driveway weighing in at sixteen stone. Ten years ago, I also had a full head of hair. Now a slight puff of wind and my combover takes flight and lifts up like Marilyn Monroe's dress over a subway grate. Ten years ago, I wouldn't have hobbled back towards the front door: back then I had two working hips and two good knees. Now, I have legs that go in one direction only and a kneecap that dislocates so often it's rented an apartment half-way down my shin. Ten years ago, my only worries were making sure I didn't book stand-up gigs on the same weekends as the football matches I wanted to watch on TV, or fretting about getting my car cleaned – now, the car is a dumping ground for chicken nuggets and melted chocolate, mixed with toddler tears.

But, most significantly, ten years ago, I had energy. I exercised. I would meet up with friends for lunch. I would do a hundred stand-up gigs a year, probably one hundred sit-ups a week. I would take the stairs in shopping centres and socialise … a lot. I would go out and stay up until the morning time. Now, I do all that except with a four-year-old alongside me demanding 'psgetti bolognese'.

Where had all my time gone? I never would've believed ten years ago that the best present anyone could give me is time. As I grow older, Chaucer's saying 'time and tide wait for no man' makes more sense every day. I only wish it was 'time and tide will wait for you as you get your shit together'.

I closed the front door and sat down on the destroyed couch. It would be the first time ever that I'd sleep in the house on my own. Usually, Tadhg wakes me at 2 am every night. I get him water, tell him a quick story or say 'no' to one of his bizarre demands. They range from 'Get me a ham wrap,' to 'I want bread and an orange,' to my personal favourite: 'Bring up all the monkeys from downstairs.'

A third small person has entered our lives in the last year, too – Seán. He has been using the corners of the leather panels on the couch as teething toys. He has devoured several of those chewy giraffes and is moving onto cowhides. At four, Tadhg is now a big brother and Olivia, at six years old, is head of the siblings. Olivia, like most girls, is smart and at any time can position her brothers on the chess board of life at will.

Now, the dynamics of family life were in full swing, but I needed a break. I'd forgotten what it was like to eat a bowl of cereal without someone wanting to put their hand in it. I'd forgotten how pleasurable it is to spend an entire day on the couch without finding a beheaded teething giraffe buried under a cushion. I'd forgotten what it was like to have a day where I did nothing. The quiet. That's the first thing that hits you … the quiet. I love the kids, but I also love the quiet.

I could even hear a lawnmower in the distance.

I turned on the TV. Then the realisation hit: I don't have to get up. I don't have to get anybody a yogurt. I don't have to deal with tears, or spilled milk, or fights over Coco-Pops. I could sit down and watch an entire programme without being interrupted or accosted. I could have a cup of tea without it getting cold. For the past five years every time I've made a cup of tea, I've ended up throwing it out because it's gone cold.

The TV blared into the silence. The sound was at 47, but I could still hear it when I turned it down to 10. That's how loud our house is with three kids under six. I remember going to Grands Prix years ago and they would hand out earplugs so your eardrums wouldn't get damaged. They should hand them out to parents when they have their first child. It's the noise kids make that nobody prepares you for.

How dreadful an irony it is that, as the human body ages, the senses deteriorate. Surely, as you get older, you need your hearing and sight to stay alive because your muscles weaken and movement slows down? Surely that would be a nice payoff, but no. I can't take the soundtracks of kids' programmes anymore either. I can't listen to *Peppa Pig* without thinking about terrible ways to bring about her consumption as breakfast. I feel like getting sick every time I hear the intro to *Paw Patrol*. For those of you unfamiliar with the programme, it's about a 'patrol' of puppies who solve problems and generally save the day. Why can't they have an episode where they save tired parents from thinking they can travel more than an hour with three small children, instead of one of turtles crossing a moderately busy road?

I can't listen to the screeching of chairs being pushed across the floor either. This process normally ends with one of them doing something that will either require a clean-up time of half an hour, or being brought to hospital. Seán, who's only one, has found multiple ways of climbing up on chairs, then onto stools, then on to his final destination: breaking a glass or being electrocuted by some household appliance. When I read about people's incredible journeys climbing Everest, all I can see, as they take their final step onto the summit, is Seán in the background pushing a chair in the snow, pointing at something he wants.

But somewhere amongst the crying, screaming and shouting, their blitzkrieg of noise, are demands and cries for help that always come just as I'm about to do something.

My top five cries for help, in descending order, must resonate in almost every house that was ever built:

5: 'Daddy, I'm stuck.'

The places where the boys get 'stuck' are unbelievable. Tadhg and Seán regularly get stuck in the fridge, the utility room, or any gap where their heads can fit, whereas if Olivia shouts, 'Daddy, I'm stuck,' it normally means me explaining what 'extravagant' means in her *Frozen* book.

4: 'Daddy, I'm hungry.'

They are always hungry, no matter how much we feed them. As for trying to make them their dinner without one of them saying, 'When is it going to be ready?' I fear anyone listening to us would think we're starving them.

3: 'Daddy, Tadhg hit me,' or, 'Daddy, Olivia hit me.'

I remember myself and my sisters playing together, but I remember the fights more. It's almost as if, over time, they've become the funnier, happier memories. Now, I see the kids playing happily together for hours on end and then all-out warfare begins. Teddies are flung like missiles. Barbies are then taken hostage. Dinosaurs are dumped in the toilet and there are tears, lots of tears, and screams, all because 'He said I was smelly'. I got so fed up one day I just let them at it and they eventually resolved it themselves by completely forgetting that they'd had a row in the first place.

Much to the annoyance of my wife, it's a tactic I use regularly.

2: 'I don't want to.'

This is a totally human and honest response from any living creature. But it can be frustrating when you're trying to get them all out the door on time for school and crèche and you hear 'I don't want to' as a reply to some reasonable request, like 'Please, Tadhg, put your trousers on.' If I'm being completely honest, I don't want to wash them, cook for them, bring them places, collect them or do everything for them every day, but I have to. One morning I got so frustrated, I said to them: 'Fine, you don't have to do anything. You can stay here today on your own and mind Seán and get your own dinner.' To which the reply came instantly: 'OK, bye, Daddy.'

1: 'Daddy, wipe me.'

Said by the first children to live in the Lascaux caves. If you think about the people who strove to make the world a better place – Barack Obama, Gandhi, Madonna or Bono – they, too, must have roared 'Wipe me', at some point in their development. This was one of the things I was most looking forward to about my week off. No nappies or bathroom time or potties.

But when it comes to noise and children, nothing tops that in the divisively named 'soft play areas' in shopping and entertainment centres. I never knew these places existed until we had kids. I most definitely didn't know they were the dominant place for birthday parties. The one thing I've noticed is that they all have similar names like 'Bounce Zone', 'Play-world', 'Go-Play-Go'. They are never called 'Nervous-Breakdown Zone', or, 'You-Will-Need-Drink-After-an-Hour-World.' My wife seems to take to these places better. She seems to have evolved an ability to rationalise the noise and to talk at the same time. She is almost like a pair of noise-cancelling headphones. Most fathers in these places congregate in a corner, checking the football results on their phones, or staring hopefully at the Tannoy system, eagerly awaiting the announcement of the presentation of a quickly devoured One Direction cake, a signal that the party is nearly over. It's not that we don't care about making happy memories for our children, it's just the noises are telling our brains, 'Get out – escape now, while your son's head is stuck in the entrance of the *Paw Patrol* tower.' It's where men like myself are herded every weekend. We don't talk. We just nod and smile to each other knowing that, while this party will eventually end, there will be more. Unlike war, there will never be a party to end all parties. Sometimes, we look at a father who has had to get off the limited seating and propel himself into the giant padded universe to rescue his crying child. We don't follow him in or give any help. We just watch as he tries to squeeze through the multicoloured batons and tackle the grappling wall to pull his daughter's fairy wings out of the ball-pit netting on the third floor. We look up and think, thank God that's not me today.

Once the chips and nuggets are eaten and the party bags that are designed to keep the sugar levels up for the night are distributed, we load our children into people carriers. Not cars. People carriers. Not a streamlined sports car like the ones that we had on posters on our bedroom walls as children, but a metal box with two, or even three, rows of seating. No child has ever had a poster of a minivan on their bedroom wall.

I decided that whatever I was going to do for the next five days, it would not involve being a 'father'. I was taking a break off from being 'Daddy'. I was still a young, vibrant, creative man with energy and vitality. I spent the next two hours sitting on the couch watching *Sky Sports News*. Eventually, after four mugs of hot tea and an entire packet of tea cakes, I mustered up the energy to send out a text to my friends. It was one I'd sent often in my twenties and thirties and then hadn't sent in ten years. It was a simple message, one that I got almost giddy with excitement sending:

ANYONE UP FOR A FEW PINTS?

I looked at it before I sent it. It was beautiful. But the most beautiful part of it was a 'few'. It had no time restriction, like the text messages of the recent past:

ANYONE UP FOR 2/3 DRINKS ON SATURDAY BETWEEN 7:30 PM AND 9 PM?

This was all-out social warfare. No next-morning hangover that I'd have to nurse while in 'Kidz-Jumpy-World'.

My first-day plan was simple. I was going out to get drunk and I was going to sleep in the next day, wake up and eat a breakfast consisting of things that would knock a few years off my life. But three hours later the text replies were:

SORRY CAN'T. TAKING THE KIDS TO A PARTY AND HAVE THEM TOMORROW.
I'M IN SPAIN.
I'M GIGGING TONIGHT, SORRY.
NEED MORE NOTICE — WHAT ABOUT NEXT WEEKEND?
YEAH, WOULD LOVE TO, COULD YOU BE IN CANADA IN SIX HOURS' TIME?

CAN'T TONIGHT. CAN MEET YOU FOR LUNCH TOMORROW?

That's what you forget. Just because you have a week to put your life on hold does not mean that others have. Then I thought, why don't I just go out by myself? Up until that point, I'd never gone out for a drink on my own. Always too conscious of what others might think, now, I decided to bite the bullet.

I showered and took the train into town. I went into a hotel bar near the station where I was sure nobody I knew drank. I had been there once before and thought it would be the perfect place for a quiet pint. I'd daydreamed about going there and just having a drink. (I'd have to say, my daydreams have changed radically over the years. When I was a boy, I'd daydream about being a footballer. When I was a teen, a rock 'n' roll star. When I was in my twenties, a comedian who could fill big venues. In my thirties, it was making sitcoms and now, as I reach my forties, it's a more mundane dream.)

I walked down the stairs into the crypt-like room. It was dimly lit; the kind of bar where you'd meet to have an affair or buy classified secrets from former Soviet spies. It had plush brown leather couches and candles on the tables in old whiskey glasses. There was a drinks menu. I always find this amusing. I understand having a cocktail menu, but when they mention things like 'bottle of Heineken' or 'Guinness, pint or bottle', I always feel like saying, 'Oh, I see, you sell beer, that's interesting. I'll have one of those.'

I sat down at the counter and ordered a pint of Guinness.

'Waiting on someone'?' the barman asked.

'No,' I replied. An awkward silence followed. Normally, I'd fill it with small talk, but I didn't want to. I sat at the counter and drank three pints on my own. I wasn't feeling 'down' or 'unhappy' or 'disconnected' – I just enjoyed the silence. I was incredibly happy to be that 'loner' at the bar. I didn't look at my phone or at the TV. I just sat there quietly, loving the fact that when I asked for something, someone else would have to get it. I could see the barman making himself a cup of tea. I really wanted to ask him to get me something to see what that would be like, but I didn't. I couldn't do it to him. I saw a couple sitting at a circular table not far from me. I knew they were married and had kids because they clearly had nothing to talk about.

I hate the pressure married couples are put under to pretend they're young lovers. When you see couples in restaurants laughing and holding hands, it's not that they're soulmates and have never-ending energy for each other; it's because they are still in the 'interview' stage of their relationship. I get really pissed off when you see so-called 'experts' talk about married couples going on date nights. I remember reading an article in a magazine and one of these self-proclaimed experts said, 'Treat it like you don't know each other.' That would go well if I did that with Lorna, if we ever escaped for a night out: 'So, where are you from?' 'Any kids?' 'Any hobbies?' We know so much about each other that it is impossible to not know nearly everything.

That's why, as we get older, couples ... couple up. In this hotel bar, that's what the booths were full of: couples like me and Lorna talking to other couples. Talking about the same things – kids, property prices, holidays – only in this case, to another couple. I like to call it the 'i-couple update,' like the ones on your phone that, when they're downloaded and installed, are nearly exactly the same but with enough changes to make them interesting again. And that's what a night out with another couple is like. (I'm not sure what an Android update is like.)

After my three drinks, I was bored. I said my goodbyes to the barman and walked out onto the busy Dublin streets. It was dark now and I noticed something odd. I felt lightheaded. My breathing was bizarrely slow and as I started to walk, I was a bit wobbly. It genuinely took me a few minutes to realise I was drunk. 'After three pints?' I said out loud. I couldn't believe it. Then the realisation hit me harder than the cold air. Even if I wanted to go out and paint the town red, I couldn't. I wasn't physically able. I used to be the last one home and now I was on a train looking forward to going to bed. It was 9:45. People were only starting to go out.

By the time I got back to my house I had met someone else. I shouldn't have brought her back. I knew I'd regret it, but I couldn't stop myself. She lay on the side of the couch, saying nothing, just looking at me. I began to walk towards her. A friend of hers joined us, too. I wanted to resist, but I couldn't. My lips wouldn't hold back any longer. I devoured a bag of greasy, vinegar-laden chips and a cold can of Coke. Not Diet Coke, Not Coke Zero, just plain old lots-of-sugar Coke. Afterwards, once they'd had their way, I turned on the telly and watched the highlights of English football teams boring the life out of each other in scoreless draws. Eventually, I fell asleep on the couch.

I woke at 5:30 am with a crick in my neck and indigestion. I walked up the stairs and fell into my bed. No-one was looking for ham wraps, or water, or yogurts. I knew I'd wake up a little hungover, but I didn't care. What a shitty night out. The best I'd had in years.

I woke up groggy. I thought I would have a hangover, but it wasn't that bad. I looked at my phone: it read 07:43. Normally, if I woke at this time, I would have slept in by an hour. Getting a lie-in made me nervous. What if I got used to sleeping in for the next few days? I decided that I was not going to waste the next four days doing nothing. I got up and showered – on my own. Something that seems so ordinary was so glorious. Normally every time I shower, the kids come in wanting me to get them something or getting me to put Netflix back on for them. Then I thought: 'Why don't I take a bath?' I decided not to, as the last time I ran a bath, I had to ring Lorna to come home from work as I'd slipped a disc in my lower back getting out of it.

I sat down again on the couch. The smell of the chips from the night before and the empty can of Coke made me feel guilty. I hated the fact that I felt guilt these days about food. Every time I had an ice-cream or chips, a little white angel would appear on my shoulder and say, 'Bernard, you're trying to lose weight, that's not a good idea.'

I sat there, drinking coffee in my underpants, watching morning telly until midday. My wife hates it when I don't have trousers on. I can't explain why, but I hate wearing them. If I was in charge of the world, I'd allow people to take off their trousers wherever and whenever they wanted. It's completely normal to take off your coat, or a jumper, or even your shoes, but you take off your trousers and it's a complete social no-no. Once, I researched if there were any cultures that discarded the bottom half of their clothing and couldn't find one, except for maybe the ancient Greeks, who would train in the nip. I feel that when you put your trousers on, you're up for the day. It's official: you are going to work. But if you're in your house on your own, it's liberating just to walk around in your underpants. However, I had arranged to meet my friend, Neil, for lunch in town at 2 pm so I eventually put on trousers and headed out the door.

I met Neil in college, and he has been a friend for over twenty years. So, we didn't need any informal chit-chat to catch up when the waitress led us to our seats. He had returned home temporarily from working in New York.

'How come you're able to go for lunch?' he asked me. I explained Lorna's present to him. 'Nice, what are you going to do?'

I thought about it for a while. 'I don't know.' I actually didn't know. 'I was going to just head out to the airport and get on a plane.'

He looked at me sceptically. 'No, you weren't.' He was right. I wasn't. Then he suggested a 'staycation'. 'Why don't you visit the sights here in Dublin?'

I had a quick reply: 'Because I've seen them a thousand times.'

Then he quizzed me on how many of the tourist attractions I had actually been to: 'Have you been to the Guinness Storehouse?'

'No.'

'The National Gallery?'

'No.'

'The Botanic Gardens?'

'No.'

'The Museum?'

'Which one?'

'Any of them?'

'Well, I go to the café in the one with the stuffed animals – they have nice muffins.'

'Do you go inside?'

'No.'

'Have you seen the Book of Kells?'

'No.'

'So, you haven't done any of the tourist attractions in the city.'

'I go to the zoo.'

I decided to have a drink with my meal. This was really living on the edge. I don't ever drink during the day.

When I say 'ever' … I have recently ordered nothing but a pint of lager for my lunch. I was in London meeting a UK-based production company to talk about a project I was working on. They invited me to a nearby pub after the meeting. It was around 2 pm, so I just thought they were being sociable and filling in my day until I had to return to the airport. The British, unbeknownst to me, will have a drink with their lunch. (The Irish don't, because if we did, we wouldn't return to work.) I sat down and the waiter asked us what we would like to drink. As he went around the table most people said they wanted a glass of wine. I don't really drink wine. When I say 'don't really' … I do, but I fancied a pint of lager. I ordered it and went to the toilet. By the time I came back, one of them asked, 'Do you want to see the menu, Bernard?'

I replied, 'No, I'm grand, any lager will do,' as I thought she was referring to choosing from one those stupid craft beer menus. I did not know they were having their lunch. Our drinks arrived first and then I could see plates following. The waiter was saying, 'Who ordered the scampi?' I then realised that I was having a pint of lager for my dinner. I should have told them that I'd got confused but the truth was too embarrassing: that my ego was so large that I believed they would take an hour out of their day to entertain an unknown Irish comedian until he got the Heathrow Express to the airport.

It was the most excruciating hour of my life. Firstly, I was doing nothing to help the stereotype of the Irish being alcoholics and secondly, I really wanted a second pint but was too ashamed to ask. An innocent question like 'So, Bernard, do you have kids?' felt like an accusation. 'What does your wife do?' Well, she doesn't have a pint of lager for lunch. Eventually we said our goodbyes. To rub salt into the wound, the owner of the company said, 'Don't worry, Bernard, I'll get your drink.'

I was on safer ground back in Dublin, although Neil did say, 'Jesus, you're going all-out.'

I was a bit irked. 'I won't get a chance to do this for another while, so I might as well.' I've noticed a marked difference in conversations with my male friends as we get older. We don't really talk about relationships or kids. Most of our time is spent talking about sport or work. Every time I come home from meeting one of my male friends, Lorna asks me: 'How's his dad/mum/wife/sister/lover?' She always gets annoyed with me when I say I don't know, asking why I'd just wasted valuable time with a friend talking about nothing. I always say the same thing: 'If they have a problem, they will tell me.' Almost once a week, Lorna ends up saying to me, 'I don't want you to fix any of my problems. I just want you to listen.' I'm not actually able to do that. It's not that I lack empathy, it's that if someone is telling me about a problem, I automatically think they are looking for help.

Obviously, the part of my brain that deals with emotion must be missing because myself and Neil talked and argued over our lunch about who should manage the Irish football team and afterwards both of us felt satisfied with our conversation. When we finished up, he said, 'I might go for a drink after work if you are still in town.' I told him to text me to see but I knew instantly that I would be. We said our goodbyes, which consisted of not saying goodbye, because he wasn't waving me off at a steamy train station in the 1940s as I headed off to the Front. We don't hug or high-five each other, though we might shake hands. 'Talk later,' he said.

I decided to go to the National Gallery before I was tempted to order another drink. Firstly, because it was near and secondly, because I'd never been there before.

I like to think I understand art. I know, by even saying that, it probably means I don't. I like abstract painters like Rothko and Mondrian, possibly because I feel like I could do them myself. Rembrandts and Da Vincis, on the other hand, are amazing. They dedicated massive chunks of their lives to completing landscapes and portraits – that would be too much for me. I've always loved the idea of being an artist but lack any skill whatsoever with a paintbrush. I remember when I was five years of age in school, being asked to paint my family. We all got to work, and the teacher got one of the kids to collect them all when they were dry. She then got us to sit around in a circle and put our hands up when she presented our picture to the group. When she held up mine, she said, 'Who wasted all this paint?' It was so bad she thought someone had just blobbed paint on a page. In fairness, maybe I was just being abstract back then without even knowing it.

I walked around the first few floors and eventually got stuck behind a school tour. One of the kids started pointing at me and laughing. Then he said, 'You're wearing the same clothes as the man in the picture.' I looked over to where he was pointing and, on the wall, there was a portrait of a stout man, wearing a green sleeveless cloak lined with brown fur, with a red shirt underneath it. I was wearing a green gilet and red shirt – the same colours, but not exactly the regal dress that the fella in the picture was sporting. Then the little boy beside the first child said, 'And you have a big belly like him as well.' All the kids laughed and then were scuttled off to the next room.

I took a step back and looked at the painting. It was nothing special. Just a bog-standard portrait of a rich man from the 18th century. I read the little white card beside it: PORTRAIT OF JOSEPH LEESON, LATER 1ST EARL OF MILLTOWN (1711–1783) BY POMPEO BATONI. On closer inspection, the 1st Earl had the strangest hair I've ever seen. It matched the fur exactly on the trimmings of his green cloak. It gave the illusion that either his hair had grown onto the coat, or he was wearing a fur hat, or his hair was so thick that he wove clothes from it.

As I looked closer, I realised that he was clutching his penis. There was no mistaking it. He was grasping his groin in the area under his belly. It was exactly the way Michael Jackson would, except without the sunglasses. The more I looked at it, the more I realised one very obvious fact: this man, Joseph Leeson, was fat. The kids were right. We both shared a common trait – our bellies. The Italian artist Pompeo Batoni obviously needed to paint this Irish fella in a decent light, so he got him to cup the family jewels, hiding his belly, and to wear a furry hat to hide his bald head. Pompeo was hiding Joe's mid-life crisis – he basically 'airbrushed' the Earl. Long before misguiding Tinder profiles lurked vapidly in cyberspace, Italian artists stroked the egos of wealthy fat men, who had lost the run of themselves in middle age.

The more I walked around the National Gallery, the more I realised that the walls were full of men with expanded bellies clinging desperately to younger versions of themselves, knowing that they will never have the same upper body strength. Men just like me. Manopausal men.

Every man who was standing up in his portrait was wearing a cummerbund, or his stomach was draped with a layer of clothing. Half of them weren't with their families but were standing beside their horses or holding them by the reins. It would be the equivalent of a picture of me standing beside a sports car while holding my stomach in. It was comforting to know that whatever loss of youth I was feeling, someone had felt the same well over two hundred and fifty years ago.

I spent about two hours walking around the gallery and decided it was time to leave my brethren. I thought about the rest of the places I could go that Neil suggested at lunch, but I had had enough of culture for one day and ventured forth into a place that had been forbidden for so long to me. The grown-up cinema. I was trembling with excitement, knowing that I was going on my own. When I got there, it was about four o'clock and I had two choices of film: *Captain Marvel* or an art-house film based on the paintings of Vincent Van Gogh. Being such a culture vulture, I decided on *Captain Marvel*. As I went into the lobby, I noticed a family with a small child beside the Ben and Jerry's ice-cream counter. They were going to the film adaptation of *Dumbo*. I walked over to get a small tub of Phish Food (possibly a large tub) and the little girl looked at me. 'Are you going to the cinema?' I said.

'Yeah,' she roared back.

Her mother, who was trying to carry three large drinks and ice-creams, said, 'It's her first time, isn't it, Maria?' I thought instantly about all the wisdom I could pass onto this couple but instead I just opted for 'Good luck.' It might be an unusual blessing for just going to the cinema, but they had no idea what lay ahead of them. Given the right amount of time I could have given them a TED Talk entitled:

What To Expect When You Bring Your Kids To The Cinema

Please welcome to the stage, Bernard O'Shea.
Round of applause.

Thank you, thank you. Ask yourself a question. When was the last time you went to the cinema alone? If you are like me, it was probably ten or fifteen years ago. Now, ask yourself, why – is that? Are you like me and millions of other men and women aged between thirty-five and forty-five who have children under six? If so, the last five films you probably saw were: *Thomas and Friends, Peppa Pig, Frozen, Trolls* and *Aladdin*. (*Wait for audience laughter to fizzle out.*)

But seriously, when was the last time? What film was it? For me it was over ten years ago when I saw *There Will Be Blood*. I never realised that *there would never be* a time again when I would get to sit alone on my own at the cinema. Years would pass before I could enjoy a drink on my own without having to share it, maybe even have an alcoholic drink before or afterwards. According to a recent study that was never carried out by anybody, over thirty per cent of all adults say going to the cinema is one of the most enjoyable things to do if they have spare time. But alas, once children come along, that enjoyable activity fades away like the display on a cheap digital watch that's been left out in the sun for too long.

So, let us ask ourselves a different question. Why do we bring our kids to the cinema? Do we want them to enjoy the excitement and pageantry, the inspiration that motion pictures can imbue in their imagination? Or is it simpler than that? Is it, as the Disney Corporation would say, just 'To make people happy'? Fundamentally we know it's because we couldn't be arsed to bring them anywhere else. As a thirty-nine-year-old man who sees forty coming at him with less agility than a rusty tank on a salt plain, I bring them because of the three S's: sugar, silence and screen time. Also, because we live in Ireland, where any activity that is planned outside in advance is punished by Jesus by making it rain. Thus, the refuge of the cinema is where our little caravan of dampness pulls up every bank holiday weekend and at least once or twice a month.

I'm not here today to debate the rights or wrongs of bringing your children to the cinema. I'm here to help. I've put together a simple guide on how to survive. There are five easy rules to follow that I promise will make your visit to the silver screen a pleasant one. As you have probably worked out by now, I use the term 'silver screen' because I've run out of options for the word 'cinema'. (*Again, wait for audience laughter to fizzle out.*)

(*The screen will appear behind me like a cinema screen and it will count down the five rules as if it's counting down the intro into a film.*)

5: Don't arrive early.
This is vital. If you arrive early, it allows your children to ask continuously, 'When does it start?' It also allows them to change their minds about going at all. If this happens and it's raining, you're in big trouble, as you will open the

day by telling them 'Put that down' in various shops in the centre.

4: Let them eat sugar.

Sugar, especially for children, gets a bad name. It has been blamed for wars, diabetes, chronic obesity and mental disorders, yet nobody mentions the benefits. It allows you to enjoy four to five minutes of peace while your child munches on white gold. It also allows for a brief period of happiness where all your inadequacies as a parent melt away in their mouths.

3: Get to know the location of the toilets.

This is a vital marker in your child's movement throughout your cinema experience. Locate them. Make a mental note that you will be visiting them regularly – approximately six to seven times per film. Understand that this is an adventure for your child and a break for you, unless …

2: Don't get involved with the film.

On a recent outing to see *Toy Story 4*, I was so immersed in the movie that I was constantly angered by my children's insistence on getting up and going out to relieve their bladders. I kept missing vital parts of the plot and it almost felt like I was there for my own pleasure.

1: Bring change.

A change of clothes, yes, but more importantly, coins. One of your children will have no interest in the film but will have an almost intense relationship with one of the moving rides in the foyer. Five euro should cover you for half an hour while they ride in Peppa's car. This will give you time to check your Instagram or daydream about being single, drinking cold wine on a balcony in Florence, driving a Formula 1 car or going to the toilet on your own.

And finally, if you ever get the chance to go to the cinema on your own, take it. It might be another fifteen years before you get the chance again.

Take applause. Bow. Exit stage left.

I sat into the half-empty theatre to watch *Captain Marvel*. The film was based on the original comic book heroine, Carol Danvers. Interesting, I thought, as I took a slurp of my Coke and a spoon of Phish Food at the same time. However, I instantly fell asleep. It might have been the tough night I'd had the night before or maybe all my walking around the gallery, but I always fall asleep anyway. If I'm in a warm, dimly lit place, I nod off.

I woke up later, not startled or confused, just rested. I took out my phone to check the time and I had gotten a text from Neil:

WANT TO GO FOR A FEW PINTS?

Six pints later, we ended up in a nightclub. We did it almost ironically. We were following the less traditional pilgrimage of middle-aged men. Whereas some people thrive in finding themselves on the Santiago de Compostela, we were finding ourselves in an overcrowded, overpriced former shoe shop pretending we were twenty again. We knew we were going to be the oldest people in the club. It was the first time in my life where the bouncer was younger than me. At the door, I asked him, 'Do you want to see ID?'

He didn't get my joke and said, 'No, you're OK'.

Years ago, I would look like at men like me and think, 'What are they doing in here?' We were two men in our mid-life looking aimlessly at a dance floor. We were the only people there in trousers and shirts. We were the only ones sitting down. The music was 'too loud' and 'shite', something I've got used to saying in the last few years. But I knew I needed to be there. I knew that, as I looked at what most people were wearing and thought, they're going to get a chest infection. As the hormonal boys stumbled about with their creatine-fuelled biceps and T-shirts that had writing on them, I knew I just needed the confirmation that my red corduroy shirt and green sleeveless jacket weren't now, nor ever would be, in vogue. In a reversal of the usual adage that I wouldn't check myself into a nursing home because I'm too young, here, I didn't need to check myself back in because I was too old.

The realisation that this wasn't for me anymore, combined with someone asking Neil, 'Are you a cop?' led me to the inevitable decision: 'I'm going home.' And, at 12:30 am (proud of myself that I'd stayed out past midnight) me and my big belly got a taxi home. I stumbled onto the couch and turned on the TV. The telly must've known I was drunk because it popped up a heading: 'Movies Just for You.' I flicked through them and saw my boyhood favourite, *Back to the Future*. I gave Apple Inc €8.99 and sat back to enjoy a classic. I woke again at 5:30 on the couch. I'd missed two feature films, found my doppelgänger in an art gallery and realised I was officially old. Not a bad day.

DAY 3

I am a member of a gym, but I have the decency to rarely ever go there. However, after my near-death experience having six drinks and staying out after midnight, I needed to sweat the alcohol out of me early if I was to get anything from my third day of freedom. I drove to the gym, which is only a mile and a half away from my house.

It's a constant bone of contention between me and my wife. 'Why don't you walk to the gym? You'll get more exercise doing that than you would at it.' She was right. I normally go for a swim (a lap or two) then sit in the steam room for twenty minutes – in total, I've been to my gym twice in the last year. Once was to shower because the water had gone in our home, the other time was to exercise, but I soon gave up as there were topless men 'spotting' each other on the machines, so I decided to go straight for the steam room and bypass the swim rather than flaunt my fat.

I notice it's a thing now to have 'gym buddies' and that there's pressure for guys to have 'god bods' and six packs. The only man who had a six pack when I was growing up was Peter Andre, but he had the decency to be a pop star and not an everyday man, thus he was an anomaly, like Schwarzenegger. The societal pressure men feel nowadays is the pressure women have felt for hundreds of years. Walk into any newsagent and the magazines are as full of ripped men as they are of female models. However, it's the internet that's the New Testament for Millennials. Instagram and Facebook are full of ripped men shouting, 'Hey, you, want to lose weight fast and gain muscle?' None of the methods work. I know this because I've tried them all. In the last ten years I've signed up for at least fifteen to twenty of them. They all involve two main ingredients: time and dedication, neither of which I possess.

Now, as I sat in the steam room, drinking my bottle of Lucozade Sport, which is designed in conjunction with top athletes to aid the hangovers of lazy men, two 'gym buddies' walked in. From their conversation, it was as if they were a different species to me.

'So, are you heading to the CrossFit class tomorrow?'

'Nah, I think I'll just keep doing the arms programme.'

'That the one from your PT?'

'Yeah, she'll know if I don't finish it.'

PT. Personal Trainer. The only time I hear PT now is when we have a parent-teacher meeting to go to. I did go to a brilliant personal trainer for six weeks a year ago and I lost weight and felt great, but again, the Sword of Damocles of work, kids and time made me give up. As I looked across at the two Millennials, neither of whom looked as if he needed a personal trainer, I felt a bang of guilt that I possibly should have kept going. But they were about twenty-three at the most and probably had the metabolism of cheap polyester.

'You heading out tonight to Mark's party?'

'Nah, I'm not going to drink until I'm finished the semester. What about yourself?'

'No, I'm not either. I promised myself I'd get a 2:1 and that's what I'm going to do.'

'I'm screwed if I don't get a 2:1. I mean, it's not the end of the world, but it's not a great way to start a career off,' the other one replied.'

What was he talking about – a 'career'? I wanted to tell him, 'Hey, I don't have a "career". Most people don't have one – they have a mortgage.' But I really wanted to tell them they should go out to Mark's party and get hammered.

'Sarah and I are saving to go to Brazil for the summer anyway,' said the first guy.

'Cool, Brazil. I went to Argentina backpacking with Seán and Will last year. Amazing experience.'

I'm sick to the teeth of hearing that word 'experience'. They'd been beginning to annoy me, but this sent me over the edge. Surely if you go seeking an experience, you will never find it. Why are Millennials so infatuated with experiences? I've had 'experiences' – I just call them great stories that happened to me when I was drunk. I remember a taxi driver told me once that he and his brother had bought a horse when they were drunk and went to collect it that night in Longford. It turned out to be a random horse in a field and they returned it the next day. He didn't say: 'Here, buddy, let me tell you about a great experience I had.' He said, 'I've a great one for ya.' Maybe Millennials have better mental and physical health and worldly knowledge, but I fear their curated lives will result in none of them accidentally stealing a horse.

'There's so much back work to get through on the course. I just don't think I'll finish all the modules,' the guy continued.

'I got really freaked last week,' his friend said, 'so now, I just stick in the earphones every morning and do a quick twenty-minute meditation.'

'Oh, you using Headspace?'

'No, I use Calm. I actually signed up for the premium.'

There it was. The one jewel that I lusted after. The ability to meditate. I had downloaded those apps they were talking about. I'd found them impossible. Firstly, where was I going to find twenty minutes of quiet in my house with three screaming kids and a wife who will burst in the door if she thinks I'm taking a nap in the middle of the day? Secondly, I just think a lot of it is quite frankly bulls**te.

As I drove home, I thought about what I had been doing when I was 23. I was living in a bedsit. I had no money. I had no career opportunities and I was drinking like a fish. What advice would I have given myself? I got back to my house and for the first time in two days, I really missed the family. Then I rang Lorna and I could hear them screaming in the background and I soon returned to my new normal. I sat down at the kitchen table and opened the laptop. I was about to watch car videos on YouTube but for some reason,

I decided to write a letter to my twenty-year-old self instead. I don't know why I did it. Maybe it was because of listening to the Millennials at the gym but possibly it had more to do with falling asleep during *Back to the Future*.

Bernard,

You are 23, unemployed and living in a bedsit. The most important things in your life right now are drinking, stand-up, rent and football. In less than ten years they will be replaced by kids, sleep, family and football. You are going to be married. I know – hard to believe. Who in her right mind would marry you? You are also going to have three little people relying on you for their every need. Now, you probably don't have enough money for the rent this month because you have drunk it all. You will never have a job, Bernard, and guess what? That's OK, because you will eventually get better at stand-up. You will work in radio and telly and write books. It sounds unbelievable because you once ate your dinner in bed and ended up sleeping for two days straight. But I know you would like an easier life right now, so listen to me. I'm not going to give you some life-affirming advice because your life will never be affirming. There will always be bills, deadlines and tax. That's a pain in the hole by the way … tax and VAT. You will never understand them, just learn to live with them.

So, here are a few things that will drastically change your life right now and for the future:

You are not missing out on anything. I know you hate staying in, but believe me nothing happens when you go out, and you will only remember a handful of nights out.

Sleep. I know. Everybody gives you a hard time about how much you sleep but you will not believe this. In a few years' time you will get little to no sleep.

Maybe don't drink as much. You could go out tonight and drink for the night, but soon, after two or three drinks, you'll be fast asleep.

Start going to the gym and running. You are thin now and you don't need to work out but believe me, between 30 and 40 years of age, you will put on five stone. If you start running regularly now, you won't have to run in the middle of the night when you're older or buy XXL-size clothes online.

Work just a little bit harder. You have no idea how much energy you have now, so use it. Just concentrate and do 10 per cent more work. It will pay off later.

And finally, get out of that bedsit – it's dreadful.

Yours,

Bernard

That night I went to bed at 9:45.

DAY 4

I woke the following day with much more energy. I wanted to do something productive. I decided on a whim to lift some weights. I went up into the attic to get out my kettlebell. I used to go to kettlebell classes but stopped and now use the kettlebell I'd bought primarily as a doorstop or as a weight to stop the wheelie-bin lid from opening. As I looked around the attic, I noticed the bags of clothes that didn't fit me anymore, but I'd thought that someday I might lose enough weight to fit into them. They were at least ten years old. Then I started to rummage. I found two ab machines, a bass guitar and amp, an electric guitar amp and then all my old triathlon gear. I had swimsuits, helmets, cycling shoes, even sweatbands.

Then I noticed a box with folders in it. I didn't remember seeing it before. When I opened it, it was full of old documents: old college results, medical reports, flight tickets, lanyards from festivals – basically, my twenties in a box. There was also the box my mother had given me when we moved into the house. She had kept papers and old press cuttings she thought 'looked important' at home for me and because I now had room to store them, she'd given them to me. As I went through them, I was literally going back decades. My Leaving Cert and Junior Cert results, old guitar magazines . . .

Then I saw an old A4 binder with the word 'Songs' written on it. I opened it and it smelt of damp and adolescence. It sucked me back to when I was fifteen, writing songs with my 'band'. Whereas some teenagers write bad poetry or keep a diary, I had hundreds of song lyrics with chord patterns written above them. Not alone had I labelled them with the keys and tempo, I had also put down what album they would go into and in what order. My secondary-school band only ever recorded cover songs and maybe one original (I had to beg them as they weren't very good) on an old tape recorder. The titles of the songs on the album were cringeworthy. However, my favourite had to be Album 1, which sounded like I was going through a rebellious Led Zeppelin phase to say the least.

Album Title: *The Ghost Shall Not Pass*
Track 1 – Hidden covers
Track 2 – In and out with Mr Nice
Track 3 – You bomb, I destroy
Track 4 – I'm in love with pain. You are in love with the same.
Track 5 – Cat
Track 6 – Let's be honest, I hate you
Track 7 – Sunshine
Track 8 – Acid tears, crocodile rain

Track 9 – This is about you
Track 10 – Track 10
Track 11 – I want to be in the Pixies
Track 12 – ( ) Blank Spaces

Then, joy upon joys, I found the lyrics for all of them. However, the most humiliating and funniest was the final track, 'Blank Spaces'. Strap yourself in because this gets deep:

Blank spaces eliminate faces
In the crowd there is no noise
How do you see with no eyes for me?
I take temptation to the ground
Blank spaces cruel places
The noise now turns around
Looks into the silent you
And carves tunnels in the ground
Time waits for no man
No woman waits for time
Now is the lesson we have learned
Burn the fire to the ground
Chorus:
Everyone wants a chorus we can sing to, we can sing to
Nobody wants the truth we can bleed to, we can bleed to
Every time we laugh every time we cry
Understand this: we lie

I started laughing in the attic. What did this mean? I had either just written down nonsense or copied it off the Smashing Pumpkins. I dragged down the electric guitar and amp and plugged them in. It was the first time I'd ever plugged in an electric guitar in the house and probably the first time since

I'd left college. I slammed on the distortion and the noise was loud and it felt great. I was a rock star with a mortgage and kids and for twenty minutes, I played really loudly, until I realised my neighbours must be going mental. I turned it down and played for at least ten hours straight. I'd forgotten how much I loved playing the guitar just for the sake of playing it. I didn't have to write anything for a stand-up tour or for a sketch; I just played it for the love of it. Skipping meals, not realising it had turned dark and forgetting that anything else existed.

I looked at the lyrics of 'Blank Spaces' again and smiled. What would my album be today? I thought of a few titles: 'Middle-of-the-Road-Aged Man', 'Hair-liner', as in a play on 'Headliner', 'Expanding Waist of Time', and then I thought, *Manopause,* what a perfect title for an album. I'm a man. I'm going through my male menopause and my metabolism is on pause. I started strumming a honkey-tonk *Rolling Stones* riff and writing down lyrics for my new epic title track:

Manopause is what's happening me
Very soon I'm going to be forty
I'm taking supplements for nearly everything
My waistline's expanding and I'm retiring
My taste in music is getting narrow
The last thing I test drove was a wheelbarrow
Most of my clothes are beige by choice
I'm not big-boned, it's just my mid-life crisis

In the blink of an eye, I'll be in a nursing home
My kids better visit me
In the blink of an eye, I'll be six feet under
And eventually everything will be free

It wasn't much of a hit, but I put it in with the rest of the lyrics. I packed all the boxes away again and stuck them back up in the attic with the rest of my hopes and dreams. I kept the kettlebell. Maybe I might surprise myself and do a bit of exercise.

DAY 5

It was the final day of my present. I had done nothing with my previous four days off. There were a million and one things I had planned on doing: I wanted to start flying lessons, drive a race car, read *War and Peace*, and all I did was get drunk, fall asleep and write a song about getting old.

I had warned Lorna off organising any kind of party for me. I hate surprise parties. I don't like the idea of people just showing up to surprise you because you managed to live for a prolonged period of time. I never thought that much about turning 40, but it seemed to be a bigger thing for the people around me than for myself.

I thought about getting into the shower that morning. Knowing that it would be a long time before I would get to wash on my own again, I ran a bath. I hate baths, but I ran one because it seemed to me the quickest way to achieve some form of luxury until the family returned home. I missed them. In fact, I really missed them. I knew it would also be the last time I could rifle through Lorna's bathroom cabinet and try all her creams without being caught. I threw a bath bomb and bath oil into the tub. Soon I was parboiling in my little homemade spa retreat.

I got bored quickly. So, I grabbed my phone and after it fell into the water twice, I decided that maybe it wasn't such a good idea. Then I did what people have done for thousands of years . . . I read the ingredients on the backs of the shampoo bottles. Every bottle used the words 'luxurious', 're-invigorating' and 'replenish'. After I trawled through every bottle, I found that the word 'replenish' was written on nearly every single item in the bathroom. That's what we want, I suppose, when we buy a simple bottle of liquid soap in the supermarket. We don't just want it to clean us, we want it to 'replenish' us. It's a fantastic word for the cosmetic industry because it doesn't promise to make you younger or live longer, it just promises to make what you have now better and to put back in the things you are missing, to replace the youth that has just leaked out of you, like water dribbling out of a clear plastic bag with a goldfish in it.

There was only one bottle that didn't have the word 'replenish' written on it. It was a bottle of St Tropez Bronzing Mousse with Enriched Vitamins. I never have been able to tan. I have extremely fair skin. I like the sun; it just doesn't like me. I started to think about how they chose that name: 'St Tropez'. It conjures up images of the south of France, fast cars and faster lifestyles. I can't imagine bottles of 'Castledermot' or 'Ballycumber' fake tan selling in their droves.

I squeezed out a little bit and rubbed it onto the back of my hand. It glistened a little bit but mostly it gave my pale white skin a decent texture. I then did the other hand to match it. Then each arm. Then my chest. Then my neck. Then my face. Within fifteen minutes, I had covered every inch of my body except my back. I looked at myself in the mirror and I definitely looked thinner. The colour wasn't too heavy either. It just looked like I'd been on holidays for a few days. I looked and felt good.

I decided, for my last day of freedom, that I would clean out my wardrobe. It was full of clothes that didn't fit me anymore. I had three suits that I'd kept because I promised myself that I would lose enough weight to fit into them eventually. I had T-shirts that were large in size that I could now barely get over my head as I had ballooned to an XXL over the last two years. I counted twelve pairs of trousers that no longer fitted me, and countless football tops, many of them still in their packaging.

I filled two black refuse sacks with discarded clothes. I put them on the weighing scales in the bathroom and they weighed just over two stone. Then, for the first time in months, I weighed myself. I hate weighing myself. It's like looking at your bank balance: never as good as you thought it would be. I stripped off because I didn't want the weight of my jeans and shoes to contribute to my years of heaving Häagen-Dazs down my gullet nightly. I got a genuine fright. I stepped off the scales thinking it had to be wrong. I stepped up again. Same result. I was sixteen stone four pounds. It was the heaviest I had ever been in my life. I walked back into the bedroom to get my clothes and I felt depressed. Then I caught a glimpse of myself in my wife's full-length mirror. My entire body was plastered in a streaky brown mush. I ran and found the bottle of St Tropez. I read the back of it again and there it was: 'Will darken after time'. I looked like a withered handbag. I was really, really brown – almost as if I'd just been freshly plastered by a slurry spreader.

I got back into the shower, but it just wouldn't come off me. I even tried mixing small amounts of bleach into the shower gel and it wouldn't budge. I eventually gave up. I sat down on the top of the stairs beside the two bags of clothes. I grabbed my phone and googled: 'how to get fake tan off'. It came down to two basic principles: exfoliation and steam. So, I ran another bath. I got a bag of sugar from the kitchen and mixed it in with a bottle of washing-up liquid and began to scrub myself. A bottle of Fairy Liquid, a half-pound of sugar, three baths and two hours later, I had gotten most of it off. I stuffed the two bags of clothes into the boot of my car and headed to the charity shop. It was closed by the time I got there.

I spent my last day doing nothing, only finding more ways to waste my own time. When I returned home, Lorna's car was in the driveway. What had I done with my five days? I'd missed her and the kids, but I knew I'd never get an opportunity like this again, or at least, for another while.

I walked into the hall and the kids rushed out, screaming, 'Daddy!' They gave my legs a tight squeeze.

When I went into the kitchen Lorna greeted me with the words, 'Where is all the sugar?'

When it was Lorna's birthday, even though she's five years younger than me, I decided to give her a present equal to the one she'd given me. However, I knew she didn't want to go away for five days on her own. Why? Because I asked her, and she said no. This was primarily down to her fear of me allowing the children to do whatever they wanted for five days – and because she isn't in the throes of a mid-life crisis. I knew from past experience that she had no interest in perfume and jewellery, or anything that might be defined as a present that can be bought in a shop. It has consistently been a bugbear of mine, as she is the hardest person on Planet Earth to buy a gift for. She refutes this. For the past few years, she has told me what to buy her and I normally buy the complete opposite to try and 'surprise' her. This has never worked.

Then an amazing idea came to me while we were fighting about – no, talking about – putting together a rota for cleaning the house. The rota issue has become a perennial one in the house over the last five years. Firstly, a little historical background to what I like to call 'Rotagate'. Lorna has consistently argued for a rota for house chores. I argue that I do most of the housework anyway and Lorna says that she does more. It's as simple as that. She has, however, control issues over who does up the rota. My wife is an accountant and she lives and breathes Excel spreadsheets and order. Past versions of the rota have always been skewed in her favour, to say the least. I have my suspicions about accountability and fairness and have long clamoured for a judicial review of any further publications. She just remarks, 'You don't want one because then you will have to do your fair share of housework.'

I completely and utterly deny these claims. Here is my issue. She will not let me do any of the laundry anymore, as I won't separate the colours from the whites. I won't separate the colours from the whites, because every advertisement for detergent and washing machines tells me you don't have to. It's not laziness: it is my utter belief in advertising. That's my story and I'm sticking to it.

I have produced several rotas myself, but they have been squashed before any consultations. I've pushed heavily for a week-on, week-off system. Lorna has shut this down because 'You will do nothing for your week – I know you won't'. Eventually, she did a colour-coded 'supposedly' fair rota that substituted my lack of laundry acumen for extra floor-mopping duties. I was having none of it. So, for the last five years when any argument would arise over housework, she would always announce, 'I wanted a rota, but you said NO.' The rota is by far the most divisive issue in the house.

Nagging is another issue. The word itself has become contentious. I reckon that if I'm being asked to do things by my wife again and again and again, 'nagging' is the best word I can use to describe it. But saying the word to my wife is her kryptonite – it sparks fury mode, so I'm very cautious about using it. 'I'm not nagging you, Bernard, I'm just asking you to do something,' is her usual response.

Lorna also has a knack of asking me to do one thing and then immediately asking me to do something else. For example: 'Bernard, will you take out the recycling bins?' (as I'm just about to do it). Then she will say, 'Can you turn the dryer on again?' When I respond with 'Let me do this first' it results in … dare I say it … nagging.

So, for her birthday present I decided to completely bypass any mention of rotas or nagging. Instead, I decided that for an entire week, I would become a Yes Man. I would become a surrendered husband, completely and utterly at the mercy of her every command for a whole five days. Whatever she wanted me to do, I would do it.

I wrote out on a piece of white paper:

I, Bernard O'Shea, will be at your beck and call for the next five days. I surrender completely and utterly to you. Regardless of what you want me to do, I will do it. Your wish is my command. I cannot say no. Two exceptions. I won't eat butter or touch a rat.
Signed: Bernard

To make it look more official and as if I'd gone to some effort, I presented it in a frame.

On the morning of her birthday, myself and the kids brought Lorna breakfast in bed and I wrapped the framed note to make it look more gift-worthy.

When she opened it up there was a classic Lorna reaction: 'Yeah, you are not going to do that.' For the next few hours, she refused to accept that this was her present.

'I didn't get you anything else,' I said. 'I'm serious – this is your present.'

She looked at me sadly. 'OK, Bernard, OK.'

Later in the day, Lorna asked, 'Will you unload the dishwasher and hoover the kids' bedrooms?' I had prepared for this. I was half-way into a sandwich and had just made a cup of tea. Was this a test? Was she expecting me to say, 'Yeah just let me finish my tea because I haven't had a hot cup of tea in five years because every time I make one, someone asks me to do something?' The reply she got was 'Yes'.

I went to get the hoover straight away. 'You don't have to do it now,' she said, but I was determined to be slavish to a fault. 'You ask, you get,' I said. It took me over half an hour to do both jobs. When I went downstairs after hoovering, she said, 'We're out of baby wipes and bin liners.'

I wasn't about to say, 'Ohhhh, I just unloaded the dishwasher and hoovered for GOD'S SAKE'. Not this time. 'OK, I'll go out for them now,' I said.

As I headed out the door, I was expecting her to say something … anything. I turned the key in the door, slowly expecting at least a thanks. I thought, that's what she would expect me to want, so I just went about my task, unashamedly angry. When I arrived home, she was on the phone to her friend. I was expecting her to be hysterically laughing down the phone, 'You won't believe what he got me,' but there was nothing.

Three more jobs were asked of me that evening: to tidy up the back garden, to clean the counter tops in the kitchen and finally, the one job I was dreading … to give the kids their baths.

I hate giving the kids their baths. Normally it results in one of them (no names) screaming because they've got shampoo in their eyes, but they won't let me wash the suds out their hair. I keep telling them that if I don't, their scalps will be itchy for days. I can vividly remember my mother holding down my head as she tried to put an egg cup of water over my crown to flush out the shampoo. There has to be something in my DNA that makes me enjoy the concept of water but immensely dislike the reality of it. A bath is also supposed to calm children down at night before bedtime. Again, it must be our faulty genetic code because it has the complete opposite effect on our kids. Bath time means midnight-sleep time.

Still, I managed, and, after their bath, Lorna asked me, 'Can you put them to bed as well? I'm going for a walk.'

I was now, according to my neurological handbook, officially pissed off. I wanted at least a 'thanks' and now I had to put them to bed.

By 9:15, all of them were asleep. I headed downstairs and Lorna was watching TV. 'I'd love a bag of chips,' she said.

I was just about to tell her she could get them herself when I remembered 'no saying no'. I put on my jacket and headed out the door. All I could think of now was, why I didn't say I'd be her slave for just one day?

On the second day of being a man-slave, my true love said to me: 'Can you go to the sorting office and pick up two missed deliveries?' On the way there, I got a text: Can you also put AdBlue and diesel into my car and get it washed? (AdBlue is an additive you use in diesel cars. It's essentially ammonia and it's used to bring down the CO_2 emissions. Ammonia is also present in urine and I can't help but giggle to myself every time I have to buy it that I'm actually buying wee.)

Now, I realised I was in too deep. There was no way of getting out of this deal. A deal I had invented and officially formalised in a written, framed present. This is how people do stupid things. This is how people who design human-sized bird wings jump off roofs and die. They say, 'I will fly,' then they have to go through with it. I was Icarus except before I took off, I declared, 'Just to let you know, I plan on flying into the sun.' I hadn't been tricked into giving my wife this present. She had made no overtures as to what she wanted.

I started to investigate why I'd offered it. Maybe, deep down, I thought I wasn't actually helping out enough. But then I defended myself because I do help out enough. Then I thought, am I desperate for her love and attention? Again, I refute that because plainly and simply, I'm not. I can go for long periods of time without love and years without attention. There was no Freudian avenue that I could follow that would lead me to the answer as to why I'd done this.

Then, as I arrived in the car park of the sorting office, the realisation hit me. I wasn't trying to repay her for all her hard work; I wasn't trying to even up the gift-giving scales, because she'd given me five days off for my 40th birthday. I wasn't trying to be imaginative or romantic. No, I gave her this gift because I never fully believed she would take advantage of it. First lesson learned: don't give a gift you don't actually *want* to give.

I stood in the queue in the sorting office and by the time I got to the counter, I was informed that I couldn't collect the items because the person who they were intended for needed to sign the form. I explained that it was for my wife but to no avail: 'She needs to sign it, buddy,' I was told. I then had to head back to the house and get her to sign it.

'Did you get the AdBlue put into my car and get it washed?'

I looked at her, hoping my expression would convey the essence of 'How do you think I would have been able to do that in such a short space of time?'

'Well, did you, Bernard? Yes or no?'

I snapped. 'No, I didn't, how do you think I would be able to do that? I had to stand in the queue for nearly half an hour and it was your mistake for not signing it. What do you want me to do – get the car washed or pick up your parcels?'

The answer was no more than I expected: 'Both, Bernard … both.'

So, I decided on my way back to the sorting office to buy the AdBlue in a massive DIY home store, before going to collect Lorna's packages. I've never been a fan of hardware shops, especially the massive ones. More and more gigantic superstores open every week and, for the life of me, I cannot understand why. I'm not into DIY. My terrible history in putting up shelves alone has resulted in the rule that for the sake and protection of humanity, I shouldn't be allowed within a hundred metres of anything resembling home improvement.

These places always seem to be inhabited by professionals who dive in and out quickly, like seagulls plucking fish from the sea. Then there are the well-meaning but completely inadequate consumers desperately trying to fill a void in their lives by tiling a backsplash above the sink in the downstairs toilet.

I know my wife secretly harbours a deep quasi-erotic passion for men who are handy at DIY. Actually, I know this because she has told me: 'I harbour a deep quasi-erotic passion for men who are handy at DIY.' I think it's unfair to call anyone, regardless of gender, not good at DIY simply because it's not their hobby. All those 'fierce handy people' are constantly developing their love just for their hobby, not for their significant others. Lorna constantly tells me that spending hours playing the guitar is selfish; however, if I were into wrenches and hammers instead of musical instruments there would be no issue.

Now, as I wandered around the aisles, I could see various men asking sales assistants in bright orange polo shirts questions like 'What's the best grade sandpaper for use on hardwood?' Or 'would the seventy-five-mill standard basin bottle trap give me enough ground clearance for a separate vanity unit?' Or my favourite: 'What is the main difference between the high-gloss finish and the standard-gloss finish?' Now, I'm not a homeware or paint expert, but even I would have enough gumption to possibly hazard a guess that maybe … just maybe, the 'high-gloss' finish would be 'higher' and shinier than the standard one.

This question was asked by a thin man with short grey hair, impeccably dressed in a green tweed suit and an Anglo-Irish accent. He looked like a very well-kept Samuel Beckett. However, my active eavesdropping was blown apart when the assistant, who was about four feet five inches tall and was wearing a *Star Wars* Starbucks hat with the image of Darth Vader's mask in the centre of the circular green logo instead of a mermaid, said, 'It depends, what are you painting?' Because of the hat, which screamed, 'I'm an idiot', I had been expecting an ironic, snarky answer instead of his polite reply to Samuel Beckett's doppelgänger. We all know the phrase, 'Don't judge a book by its cover' – well, I'd invented a new one for myself: 'Don't judge the shop assistant by his hat.'

I picked up my AdBlue, paid for it and headed out to the car to drive back to the sorting office. When I arrived at the top of the queue, the same guy said, 'You are back, my friend.'

'I am but this time I have the signature,' I replied.

He checked it and went and got the two items. 'Hopefully,' he said, 'we won't see you again for a while. Good luck, son.'

I just knew this wasn't going to be true. Lorna, like myself and billions of other people, now orders so much of what we used to buy in these things called 'shops' online. (If you were born after the year 2000, there is a cool YouTube video that explains what a shop was and also about something called 'cash'.) I have an Amazon problem, I know this. The only difference between myself and Lorna is that I cannot go through the Dante's Inferno that is sending items back. It's distressing and painful and filled with bureaucracy and stamps. So, I knew that what I had in my hands would somehow see its way back to its destination and I would be its factotum.

On the way back, I brought the car to be washed. I was going to use the automatic car wash but the queue for it was a least five cars deep. Across the road, however, was a hand-wash station with no queues. I drove in. A man in army overalls stopped me. 'Can you park in the centre of the wash over there and wait in the café while I clean please?' I drove the car about a hundred metres and walked into the little café beside the power washer. The young woman behind the counter asked me, 'Do you want valet as well or just a wash?'

I wasn't sure but because I'd never been asked such succinct, clear questions, I said, 'Both please'.

She pointed at a coffee machine: 'You can have coffee while you wait . . . [and then the most important bit] and watch.' She went outside and told the guy I wanted a valet as well. He nodded and they went about their business. What was this magical place? The woman didn't try any banal chit-chat and I could see the man hard at work cleaning the car. 'It's thirty-five euro in total for clean and valet, is that OK?' she asked.

'Absolutely,' I replied. For the next 40 minutes, I watched that man clean and hoover the car, work that I was probably supposed to do myself. I sipped coffee and watched him. I flicked through a car magazine and watched him. I looked at news on my phone and now and then I would lift my head and watch him. It was beginning to become something of a voyeuristic experience. However, I couldn't quite figure out why there wasn't a queue for this car wash but there was a massive queue for an automated one that didn't do half as good a job.

Then it dawned on me. It was down to Irish Guilt. Irish Guilt is a very specific form of guilt. It's guilt about ingratitude, with a dash of utter disregard for your own happiness. Up until 1992, Irish parents were constitutionally obliged to tell children who didn't finish their dinners that 'children were dying in Africa'. This was somehow supposed to make you feel bad for having a dinner and extra bad for not finishing it. Now, Ireland is on course for being the country with the highest number of overweight people in the EU.

Irish Guilt can be subtle as well. If you listen closely to an Irish person say the word 'happy', it's usually as a negative, as in, 'I hope you're happy now,' or my personal favourite, normally said about people who've won the Lottery, 'But are they happy?' I'm pretty sure I can find the origin of this particular strain of guilt. I was told every week in Mass that 'Jesus died for your sins', and 'We are all born with original sin'. This is why every time I come close to a police checkpoint, I feel like I've done something wrong. I haven't – it's just the old original sin kicking in and the fear that I might be asked, 'Where were you on the night our Lord Jesus Christ died?'

This was the reason why there was no queue at this car wash, because Irish people would feel too guilty watching someone else clean their car. It's the same reason why people do their own DIY or garden chores. It would instil too much guilt into them to see someone else clean their gutters or mow their lawn. I, however, would always get someone else to do the jobs I hate because they'd do them better and, most importantly, the money I'd give them to do it would hide the shame and guilt buried deep inside of me. Lorna needs to realise I'm not lazy – I'm just enlightened.

When I eventually returned home, I gave the two parcels to her. 'Did you get the car done?' she asked.

'Yeah, and it's cleaned inside as well.'

'Did you do it?' Now, technically I did, as I drove it to the valet centre and paid for it, so I said, 'Yeah, just used the hoover and a bit of elbow grease.'

She opened up one of the packages. It was a roll of fabric. 'Oh, I don't like it, it's the wrong colour. Return this for me tomorrow.'

I mumbled, 'I wished I could return my present.'

'What was that?' she chirped.

'Nothing, I'll do it tomorrow.'

I decided to get up earlier to make sure I had enough time to do everything. It wasn't that I didn't do housework or look after the kids normally – it was the pressure of doing double the amount and finding the time to get it all done. So, I forced myself to get up at 5:30 am. This wasn't that unusual for me. I have been doing breakfast shows on and off for nearly a decade and am used to early rises.

There is so much on the internet about waking up at 5:30 am. Apparently, if you can do it consistently, you will become a millionaire. I did and I didn't become a millionaire – I just became burnt out and tired all the time. The one thing nobody tells you about getting up at 5:30 in the morning is that you need to be in bed by 9:30 the previous night.

This time, I went for a walk in the Phoenix Park simply because I'd also forgotten that NOTHING IS OPEN at that time. Dublin still is a relatively late riser. As a city, it really only opens its eyes around 8 am, and shops open at nine o'clock. When this is mentioned to Dubliners, they completely reject the notion. My reply is 'Try getting anything to eat before 8:30.' The walk did me good, though. To see the deer run across the main road into a different pasture and to have a completely silent background was odd in the middle of a city. Dublin is like that: you have a vibrant city but, within half an hour, you can be on a mountain or beach, or in my case, looking at deer chewing grass and wondering why you got up so fecking early.

When I got home the hall doorway was blocked with plastic bags full of children's clothes. Lorna was up and had started dressing the kids for crèche and school. 'Where were you?' she asked.

'I went for a walk. Is everything OK?' That's the usual exchange for a couple who have been together for over ten years. In fairness, if it was the other way around, and my wife went for a walk at 5:30 in the morning, I would find it odd. I added, 'Well, to be honest, I got up early because I wanted to get a head-start on the day, just in case you—'

She interrupted: 'After you drop the kids off to crèche and school, I want you to return those bags of clothes to the shopping centre.' She knew this was my biggest fear. Fear. Not dislike. Fear. I have two main fears: butter and rats, but if I was to have a third, it's returning things to a shop. I hate it. Years ago, before we had kids, Lorna asked me to return an item to a shop for her. We were in Phase One of our relationship at the time. I think all relationships fall into three phases, regardless of orientation, or even species. Animals, aliens and Australians all fall into them. Phase One is the Loving Phase. Everything your partner says is funny. You are completely and utterly head over heels in love with them. You cannot wait to spend time with them. Phase Two is Acceptance. You are beginning to see their faults but are willing to overcome them. This is the vital phase because you accept them as your significant other regardless. Phase Three is the non-returnable-item phase. I know that Lorna has looked at me so many times and thought, 'If only I could return him,' but due to the amount of time, effort and defects, the shop won't accept me back – and I'm nearly certain I had no receipt.

I hate bringing items back to shops because I never know what to say to the sales assistant. When I asked Lorna, 'Why are you returning them?' her answer was 'There is no reason, Bernard, the receipt is there. Just do it.' I knew this wasn't going to work for me. I have this aura of uncertainty about me. For a brief period in college my nickname was 'Pipkin' after the nervous rabbit from *Watership Down*. I have a weird skill of instilling doubt into the most mundane of situations, so being asked 'Why are you returning these?' is the perfect storm.

As I drove to the shopping centre, I went over possible scenarios in my head. I imagined a strict employee who would grill me on my every answer. I find it comforting to constantly imagine the worst outcome in most human interactions. The comfort comes from knowing that I will most definitely raise the threat level of a normal social interaction to DEFCON-5 in my head:

'Why are you returning these?'

My reply? 'They unfortunately don't fit.'

'So, your filthy little children have tried them on? Are you trying to return worn items to the store, sir?'

Then I try, 'The children didn't like how they looked.'

To which they'd reply, 'How they *looked?* That's no reason to return these items. I have often looked at a pizza and thought, I don't like how it looks, but then I taste it and it's OK. You have no consumer right of return just because you don't like how they look. Get out, scum.'

So, even before I entered the store, I was fully expecting a bad outcome. I walked up to the customer-service desk and I was met by a friendly lady with bright blonde hair and very striking purple eye shadow. I normally don't notice people's eyes, let alone the colour of their eye shadow, but hers was really distinctive and glittery. My brain desperately wanted to say, 'Wow, what have you done with your eyes?' But experience has tamed the impulsive toddler inside me, so I just mustered whatever confidence I had: 'I'd like to return these items, please.'

She took a look at the three large bags I had placed on the counter, sucked in a breath in and said … 'OK, no problem,' and went about scanning and clipping tags on the clothes for about five minutes. Eventually, she said, 'Do you want store credit or cash back?'

I was euphoric. I had faced my fears. I had climbed my inner Everest and was now plunging my flag into the summit. Who knew that this brave 40-year-old man would conquer such a daunting obstacle? They will talk about this day at my funeral – the day I returned something to a shop without incident. 'Cash please,' I bellowed proudly.

She went to the till and gave me the money back. I had to tell her, 'My wife will be delighted with that.'

'Oh,' she said. 'Why is that?'

I told her about my present to Lorna and my fear of returning items. She was genuinely interested and said, 'That's a great present. I'd love that.'

And then I had to open my big, ugly mouth: 'You should ask your partner for it.' There was a silence. 'I don't have a partner.' Then there was a further excruciating silence. Every inch of my soul was screaming at me: 'Say, "thank you so much for your help", and get out of the shop.' But I could feel it coming. I knew I was going to say something to make this harmless exchange a Hindenburg-level disaster. I have no idea why, but I looked at her bright-sparkly-purple eyes and said, 'I'll do it for you.'

She looked at me sternly then said, 'Ah, you're OK, I'll survive.' It was then I realised she probably thought I was trying to chat her up. I wasn't. Not that she was wasn't attractive, but in my efforts to be nice, I'd come across as being mentally unwell. I just pressed the ejector-seat button and said, 'No problem. Thank you.'

She then said, 'OK, bye now.'

Again, instead of just walking out of the shop, I said, 'Bye-bye', like a two-year-old. Christ, what man in his 40s says, 'Bye-bye'?

She said, 'OK, bye,' and unbelievably, I replied, 'Bye-bye' again. I was internally pleading with myself: 'Bernard, for the love of God, please stop saying bye-bye.' I eventually got out to the car and started discreetly punching myself in the head.

That evening, as I was bringing the kids to bed, I put the money on the kitchen counter, along with the return slip, for Lorna to see when she returned from work. I did this because I knew that when the kids fell asleep, I would fall asleep too because I'd been up at 5:30. I also wanted recognition. Like a dog bringing a rabbit to the back door, I wanted to show my owner how good I was. I was no longer hiding my complete and utter need to be patted on the head and be told 'good boy'. I tried waiting up for her. I was asleep by half-eight.

DAY 4

Saturday is taxi day. It's the day we ferry our children around to various activities, along with several million other parents. You don't even have to be specific about what the activity is: all of them neatly corral parents into a congruous anthropological group called 'dropofferpickupperwaiters'. If you were to study 'dropofferpickupperwaiters', you would see similar behaviours between all groups. Firstly, they 'drop off' their offspring at a door. This door can be the entrance to a dance class, a piano lesson, sports or even a junior Latin class. The 'dropofferpickupperwaiter' kisses the child and says, 'See you in an hour and a half.' Then the 'dropofferpickupperwaiter' leaves and has exactly the right amount of time to start something but not enough time to finish it. This leaves the 'dropofferpickupperwaiter' with a constant conundrum. Should he or she:

A: try and do something like the grocery shopping and therefore run the risk of being late, or

B: walk around aimlessly getting into queues with other 'dropofferpickupperwaiters' for coffee they don't want. Mostly they choose 'B'. This leaves them waiting for the aforementioned door to be opened, when they can pick up their progeny and ask them the same question as always: 'Did you enjoy [insert activity] today?'

What frightens me about our children's weekend activities is that they enjoy them so much it's beginning to become a massive let-down when they finish, and Daddy is there to pick them up. And you dare not miss a Saturday: if our six-year-old misses dancing for more than two weeks in a row, she threatens to ring Amnesty International. Thus, myself and my wife have been handed down a sentence of perpetual weekend delivery and collection of juveniles until they are old enough to drive themselves. Then I will demand that they take me on irritating drives to see the places of my youth and will bombard them with utterly pointless and boring stories about when I was their age.

Now, by the time the swimming, dancing and birthday parties ended it was nearly 6 pm. I was dreading what Lorna was going to ask me to do, so I didn't wait around. I cajoled the children into their pyjamas and called the nighttime express to Snoozeville. When they fell asleep, I was left with a dilemma. Risk going downstairs and be given another job or go downstairs and be patted on the head and be told 'good boy'. I decided to go downstairs.

Lorna was watching a film, so I sat down and for the first time in nearly a year, we watched it together. Not a word was spoken. We were just two jaded parents lathering their brains in Netflix. The film ended and she said, 'Will you turn off the lights?' I had no more jobs. Until she said, 'Do you know what I'd love? A proper Sunday dinner tomorrow, like the ones your mum makes.' She then vanished upstairs, knowing right well that her wish was my nightmare. It was 10:30 at night and there wasn't anything resembling the makings of a Sunday roast dinner in the house. I couldn't leave it until the morning: it wouldn't give me enough time to prepare. I knew that I had to go to the ultimate graveyard of hope on a Saturday night – a 24-hour supermarket.

Food shopping is my new going out. It's a break from the madness of a house with three kids. Those little taster counters have gradually become lighthouses of happiness and offers on baby wipes fill me with joy. But when it comes to late-night shopping, particularly on a Saturday night, you are advertising to the masses that your life is somewhat finished. For me, it's the social equivalent of putting up a billboard outside my house with a picture of me on it and the headline: 'Bernard O'Shea lives here. I have given up, people.'

At the supermarket, I wandered around the aisles marvelling at the fact I could buy a flat-screen TV at 11 pm When I was growing up, just thirty years ago, telly ended at 11 pm on a Saturday night. I was, however, one of the luckier trolley pushers in the supermarket: there was a mum out with her hyperactive toddler. Toddlers scream. That's a fact. They don't care and have no shame about it. For years, I'd see toddlers in supermarkets screaming their heads off and I'd always blame the parents. Fast forward five years and I blame the toddlers.

This particular young boy's high-pitched tones were bouncing off every hard surface and ceiling tile. I turned into the bread aisle and found the mum trying to console him, but he was apoplectic with rage, as he screamed repeatedly, 'I WANT A MILKY BAR.' I felt for her as I knew that pain only too well. But I also knew that however well-meaning you are, no-one can help in that situation. The only help you could offer her would be to say, 'Give me your shopping list and address. You go home – I'll call around later and drop it off and prepare the meals for the week.' Otherwise, you are adding flames to an already ignited fire.

There was an elderly couple staring at the bread shelf as if it were a Rembrandt painting. They collectively squeezed every loaf of bread. I watched them for about five minutes. They had a conversation about every loaf, contemplating how long it would last and how easily butter would spread across it. They were the complete opposite of the mother and screaming child. They had the luxury of having time to just squeeze bread on a Saturday night and wait for death.

The child kept screaming and the old lady said to him, 'Are you all right, little boy?'

He replied, 'I WANT A MILKY BAR.'

Her husband disappeared and came shuffling back. I could see a grave error in his hand … A MILKY BAR. I knew disaster was inevitable. He handed the bar to the screaming child. Just as he did, the mother grabbed it. 'Sorry, but he has to learn.'

The elderly woman said, 'He doesn't have to learn tonight,' whereupon the mother grabbed her child, left the trolley behind and headed out of the supermarket. I looked at the old couple, imagining the conversation, the drama that was about to unfold. Instead they just went back to squeezing the bread. The only thing that was said by the elderly woman was 'Did you pay for the Milky Bar, Pat?'

I got my stuff for the Sunday roast and headed out to the car park. I started to think about the little toddler screaming. Oh, too often has my mother regaled me with stories of how difficult we all were as toddlers. I learned a great phrase from her: 'And do you know why they do it? Because that's what kids do.' A pretty simple but wise analogy. I could understand why the mother dragged the kid out of the supermarket, but the more I thought about it, the more I understood the elderly couple's reaction. They weren't telling the child to stop crying – they were just coming at it from a different perspective: they know that the child will go to school, struggle with some things, excel at others; get jobs, lose jobs; find love and get his heart broken. He'll understand what his life is about then instantly find no meaning in anything at all. He'll see himself grow up, get older, frailer but wiser. But this is the pivotal part. That man, who I'm guessing was about 80 years of age, realised that in our tiny concept of time, one day soon that toddler will be under fluorescent lights squeezing bread, waiting for nothing. Within the blink of eye, it's gone. So, just give him the Milky Bar – because life's too short.

DAY 5

I finally got to the last day. I had decided that I was going to camouflage myself behind cooking the dinner for the first half of my day. The kids were allocated jobs, mostly washing potatoes and carrots while Lorna went for a walk. Making a Sunday dinner for the first time with the kids proved difficult as the novelty of washing vegetables soon wore off. Eventually I got them to set the table a good four hours before dinner. They were so excited to get a 'Granny's dinner' in their own home. I felt extreme pangs of guilt as I had completely lost the knack of cooking dinners. I always blame it on being time-deficient, but really, I've just become lazy.

The kids started asking me constantly, 'When is dinner, Daddy … WE'RE STARVING.'

I replied, 'Good, because if you're hungry it will taste nice. Hunger is the best sauce.' To which Tadhg shouted: 'NO IT'S NOT. GRAVY IS.'

After dinner, Lorna told the kids, 'OK, guys, I'm going to take you for a cycle.'

'Do you not want me to take them?' I asked. At this stage, I had almost given up caring after being so thoroughly hazed by Lorna's requests.

'No,' she said, 'You stay here and tidy up.'

For the twelfth time that week, I unloaded and loaded the dishwasher, a chore that I wouldn't wish on my worst enemy. I tidied up fairly quickly and sat down on the couch with a cuppa.

Deep down I'd wanted the week to be an almost religious experience, some kind of journey in which I would find out things about myself that would shock me to my core. But I didn't. I just never wanted to see the inside of a sorting office or a dishwasher again, at least for a while.

Then the realisation hit me: Lorna was just getting shit done. There was no metaphor for her, no learning curve. She saw my present for what it was – a chance to get through the pile of chores that we faced daily.

Then I got a text from her. What now? I thought. I bet she's going to send me to the dump with something or get me to rearrange things in the attic. Instead it read: Oh, by the way, I'm giving you the rest of the day off.

I texted her back: Thank you.

And there it was. The pat on the head I truly deserved.

PART TWO

Birkenstocks Man

'm beginning to think a tiny incendiary device went off in my head on 25 March 2019 when I turned 40. Two weeks later, Lorna asked me, in an almost worried tone, 'Why are you wearing khakis again? You're wearing a lot of beige these days – that's going to stain quickly.'

She had a point. I noticed that I'd stopped wearing jeans. I didn't consciously decide to do it, it just happened. I once read that the brain and body have something called cannabinoid receptors in them. They can control the flow of pain and are loosely related to the cannabis plant. Research has led scientists to think that maybe the drug could be useful in the treatment of Alzheimer's. Is it possible that when a male brain hits 40, there is some synaptic transmission that lures it towards beige trousers, ultimately restricting the memory of his youth when he could fit into jeans? Essentially, am I stoned on comfort?

It wasn't only jeans though. I started exclusively wearing shoes, having worn trainers up to that point. I'd started wearing chinos because they were smarter, with the added benefit of being comfortable, but I'd stopped wearing sneakers, even though they are comfortable too! Like a virus, it spread. Within months, I was buying jumpers. Not fashionable ones … warm ones, of the type I used to buy for my dad at Christmas with a diamond pattern on them.

But then something atrocious happened, something that raised alarm bells in all directions. On a family holiday in Kerry just four months later, I would wear (please look away now if squeamish) SANDALS WITH SOCKS.

Before you judge me and call the relevant authorities, there was a reason for my grievous sartorial error. I had bought a pair of what I thought to be fashionable Birkenstocks the week previously – just in case there would be 25 to 30 minutes of sunshine that July in Ireland. I thought I'd be able to throw on the sandals, roll up my chinos and look cool ambling along some windswept beach. I know my pale, overweight, flabby, ginger look does not now, nor did it ever, lend itself to me 'looking cool'; nor is it possible that sandals can be 'fashionable', but the older I get, the more I notice I have begun to believe advertising.

When you are young, you are more cynical, or at least I was. Half the advertisements on TV were never intended for the teenage me: cars, mortgages, free-finance couches. But now, I find they're not for the adult me either. Most advertisements are not for people who have to sit down to put on their socks. They're for people who have aspirations. My problem is that I'm mentally fit enough to aspire; I'm just not physically fit enough. Recently I've noticed that if an advertisement promises to give me back my youth, I believe it. So, when I was in the shoe shop, I saw a poster of a man throwing his child into the air on a beach. He was wearing a white herringbone shirt, buttoned-down, with a smart pair of tailored Bermuda shorts. He had thick salt-and-pepper hair. He was tanned and had a jawline that could carry two shopping bags. He looked like a guy who earns a fortune with an offshore investment bank but also volunteers at his local hospital as a doctor, putting his medical degree to use. He doesn't care what he's wearing as he throws his child into the Caribbean sunset, because he is wearing a pair of Birkenstocks.

I looked at it and thought, 'That's me.' I have never walked my kids down a beach and flung them in the air, simply because they are usually covered in white, asbestos-like Factor 70 sun cream to stop them from burning, but nevertheless, I thought, that could be me. I bought them and walked out of the shop thinking, 'I will lose 20 kg by next week and I will look like a goddam DILF.' For those not familiar with the acronym DILF, it means 'Dad I Would Like to F##k'. Bar two major banking institutions and a dislocated kneecap, the 'F' part of DILF has never been a major part of my life. I'm more of a DILY, as in, 'Dad, I Would Like a Yogurt,' or as my wife calls me, a 'DILMFBFU' or, 'Dad I Would Like to Murder for Being F##King Useless.' However, there I was, walking home with a brown leather dual-strapped pair of men's sandals.

That night, as I lay in bed watching YouTube videos on how to fall asleep, I realised I had never, up until that day, felt the need to buy sandals. Most holidays, I'd wear my shoes or runners. If I was on a beach, I'd just go barefoot. So why did I need a pair of sandals? It dawned on me that I needed sandals because I wanted to have my cake and eat it. I wanted to be the DILF on the beach, but also wanted comfort. I knew if comfort was the compromise, then style was my demise. Like wearing the jumpers and chinos, my newfound foot fetish had more to do with my inability to move than my desire to be the guy in the Birkenstocks ad. I started to say over and over again in my head, 'You just bought old age.' It was true. Old age was sitting in my wardrobe in a blue box. In fact, during the last four months, I had purchased a compendium of doddering-geriatric rags. The sandals were the icing on the retirement-home cake. I knew there and then why men my age buy sports cars and have affairs: it's not because they are selfish, it's because they come home one day and realise that in their choice of wardrobe, they have effectively made arrangements for their funerals.

That night I left the death sandals hanging off the inside of the front door. It's what I do if I absolutely have to remember to bring something with me before I leave the house. It drives my wife mental. This also helps me to remember her usual shout: 'Bernard, for the last time, stop hanging your crap on the door.' That morning the kids got to them first. Tadhg was wearing them around the house. 'I told you, stop hanging your crap off the door,' Lorna said, followed by 'Why did you buy sandals?'

I looked at the kids playing with them, like a cat plays with a dead mouse, and checked to see if they had ripped the tags off … they had. 'Well, I'm keeping them now.'

'Why did you buy them, Daddy?' Olivia asked.

'I bought them for our holiday next week.'

Lorna took one look at them and said, 'They are nice'.

I was actually shocked. 'Are you taking the piss? I was going to bring them back. Do you not think I'm a bit too young for them?'

'They are sandals, Bernard, how can you be too young for sandals?' She was right – they were just sandals.

After the kids had finished using them as hunting practice, I threw them into the boot of the car. As I did, I noticed the assortment of shoes that had built up in my boot over the years, mostly associated with failure. There were my eye-wateringly expensive hiking boots, then my waterproof trail running shoes that I'd ordered online two years before. I do not go trail running. I had a pair of brand-new state-of-the-art stabilising lightweight marathon shoes that I'd bought four years before in order to train for the Dublin City Marathon. I did not do the Dublin City Marathon. Then I found a pair of golf shoes still in their box. I did not pick up golf. My Astroturf football boots that I got to play football every Wednesday night? Well, I'd played twice, and that was six, maybe seven, years ago. I have not played football since. A pair of CrossFit shoes? I went for a month. Finally, I came across a pair of tennis shoes. I did not learn how to play tennis and, more embarrassingly, had no recollection of ever buying them. They were like a round of drink you buy at the end of the night. I had a shoe to represent every get-fit-quick scheme that I'd cultivated in my lazy, waterlogged brain.

Now, for the first time in years, I threw footwear into my boot that I knew I would wear. Depressing but achievable. Slamming the boot closed, I realised that the one major regret I had was not running a marathon when I could. Now, I apparently fall into the MAMIL category: Middle-Aged Men in Lycra. I have worn Lycra before – in my twenties and early thirties – but now, when I try on my old cycling shorts, I look like an oversize muffin, wrapped in Clingfilm from the thighs up.

I had once been genuinely close to running a marathon, but I dislocated my kneecap for the second time a month before the race. It was a painful and embarrassing story. Thirty per cent pain, seventy per cent shame.

At the time, I was living in Athlone. The town is situated in the very middle of Ireland, on the River Shannon. I was working on a breakfast radio show and in the evenings, I started exercising. I built up a decent amount of stamina and secretly started training for the Dublin City Marathon. I had run up to 16 miles and was on the last few weeks of training when I dislocated my kneecap in the middle of the town, in the middle of the day, in the middle of a girls'-secondary-school lunchtime, in the middle of Ireland.

The funny thing about pain is that you will go through any amount of it to avoid shame. I was running along when I saw hundreds of pinafored schoolgirls on the path ahead of me, so I skipped off to avoid them by running across the road and when I did I felt a pain so bad that I thought someone had stabbed me. I looked down and there, for the second time in my life, I saw my kneecap hanging off my leg. But it's amazing what a man's brain will do to avoid embarrassment – I was in agony, but I could not let myself look like an idiot in front of hundreds of schoolgirls, so I pretended to stretch in front of a nearby doorway. The doorway was directly across from a restaurant where I would frequently get my breakfast and the staff started looking out at me from the service area. Then seven million schoolgirls decided to go into the restaurant and also look directly across at me 'trying' to stretch, in unimaginable pain. Eventually, one of the staff came out and shouted across the street, 'Are you alright there?' This he did in quite an aggressive manner. I then realised it looked like I was the biggest pervert the town had ever seen. I was a man with a grimace on his face pretend-stretching across the road in front of a gathering of secondary school girls buying sausage rolls.

I was in so much pain that I let my masculinity fly away like a single dove at a tacky wedding and told one of them: 'I need help ... I've dislocated my kneecap.' Eventually, I was surrounded by a sea of green tartan pinafores all staring at my knee. There was a chorus of comments and suggestions.

'Ugh, it's disgusting.'

'My Mam is a nurse, but she's at work.'

'I think it will eventually go back in if you walk on it.'

As more and more suggestions came, I realised that teenagers are utterly idiotic. I remember thinking through the pain that they were like giant toddlers that were allowed out on their own with money and that I couldn't believe that I used to be one of them. Eventually, one of them had an inspired brainwave. She said, 'Can we bring you somewhere?' There was a hotel not far up the street, so I asked them to help me there. There I was – on a rainy day in the middle of Ireland wearing black Lycra shorts and an Ireland away jersey that barely fit me being carried by half a dozen schoolgirls up the main street of Athlone. I was in pain, but they were also in pain from laughing so hard that one of them actually broke her retainer. It's at moments like this that you realise that pride is just not worth the hassle. The only tiny bit of positivity I could get from the moment was knowing that they would tell this story to each other at a reunion and laugh. 'Remember when we carried that fat, red-haired weirdo to the Lodge years ago?' Eventually, the kneecap popped back in and I called a taxi from the hotel to my flat a few miles away.

Since that day, nine years ago, I haven't run at all. I looked at the running shoes in the boot of my car and then at my enlarged stomach, or as my daughter calls it, my 'big, big bouncy belly', and thought, 'I'm going to start running again … after the holiday.' I knew I badly needed to lose weight: I didn't need to wear a belt anymore to hold up my trousers. However, I always plan on losing weight or starting an activity *after* something. The fact that I'm a professional procrastinator helps. I can procrastinate about almost anything: surgery, work deadlines, exams, you name it and I've done everything at the very last minute. It's just handy when you can fool yourself into having an excuse for your time-wasting. This time, I made a deal with myself – when the holiday was over, I'd start running again. This gave me carte blanche to eat any crap I desired in the meantime.

However, the unexpected happened during the week of our holiday – we got nice weather. For a whole day it didn't rain in Kerry. So, imbued with the enthusiasm of ants climbing up the side of a Coke can, we burst out the door and headed to the beach. The kids were amazed that they were all wearing shorts and T-shirts. Tadhg asked Lorna, 'Mammy, do I have to wear my jumpers [not a typo: jumpers plural] today?'

Lorna replied, 'No'.

Olivia shouted, 'Daddy, you're not wearing shorts or a T-shirt.'

Olivia was right, I wasn't. That's because I'm a realist. I wanted the kids to have an amazing day at an Irish beach without dying from hypothermia, but experience has led me to know that the second we put the picnic blanket on the ground, it will rain. Not just ordinary rain either, but big, cold Atlantic bullets of rain with tiny atoms of misery inside them. Rain that hasn't made the cut to become hailstones so has that extra bit of bitterness to it. So, I was dressed as I normally would be, in jumper, navy trousers and boots.

However, two hours in and it was still glorious. Olivia asked if she could go for a walk along the beach. 'I'll go with you,' I said and then remembered my Birkenstocks. I rushed to the boot to get them. I took off my boots and put them on without thinking. For some unknown reason, I then did something that I have never done in my life before. I rolled up my trousers over my knees (by this stage I'd abandoned the jumper).

We ran down the beach and started collecting stones in her little bucket. She ran towards me and I lifted her up and then it hit me: Jesus, I'm the guy in the Birkenstocks advert. I'm that guy. The ad had come true. I was sexy, I could be an investment banker, I could be the strong, silent type. Then I could see my wife, holding our other two children, running towards me. I thought something was wrong, really wrong. Even Olivia said, 'You did something wrong, 'Daddy.'

Lorna reached me, out of breath, and did that whispery-shouting thing: 'Everyone can see your underpants and the crack of your arse.' I forgot I had no belt! My arse crack was on show to the entirety of Inch beach. But then the hammer blow. As I was pulling up my trousers, Lorna looked at my feet in utter horror. 'Jesus, Bernard … you're wearing sandals with socks.' And so I was. At the tender age of just 40, I had become the butt of all ageist jokes against men. I was the guy who people take pictures of and use as a meme on social media with ironic statements like 'Who needs condoms when you can wear sandals with socks?' The Birkenstocks ad was destroyed now.

Olivia made a valid point then. 'It will stop his feet from burning, Mum.' But when I looked at my wife, I saw in her eyes – not for the first time in her life – embarrassment. Embarrassment mixed with disgust. I sat down on the damp sand and took off the shoes, then the socks. Olivia asked me if she could have them to carry her shells in them. I rolled down my trousers and put the sandals back on again on my bare feet. I looked over at them playing on the beach. They were having a marvellous time and I was happy for them, but I felt pissed off. How many times had I sworn to lose weight? How many times had I told myself, 'When I lose weight, I'll start dressing better'? I hate the word fat, but I am. I'm overweight. I'm overweight and wear sandals with socks. I try not to care but I do.

As I write this, I'm soon to be 41. I've had a varied life and some tough experiences and got through them, but even though my family were healthy and safe and happy, I couldn't stop feeling like I'd given up on myself. I looked at my belly and thought: 'This isn't me.' As a child, I'd always been skinny and scrawny, one of those kids who couldn't put on weight. Now, the only thing I owned that fitted me were the sandals. I wasn't a DILF, I was a MAMID – a Middle-Aged Man in Denial. Denial about my receding hairline, denial about my weight, denial about my youth, denial about my sketchy wardrobe choices. I could either accept it or fight it.

I decided to fight it. That night, for the first time in ten years, I didn't order dessert. The problem was, I did for the following six nights.

THE PLAN

Ironically, nine months after Birkenstocks, there I was, still looking at my belly. But round two was about to begin. Watch out, Google, because I was about to type 'rapid weight loss' into the search bar. F##k moderation and diet and exercise; I'm going for it. I'm trying the maple syrup diet, the water diet, pills, drills, coffee enemas, the strawberry diet, the clay diet – yes, eating clay. As for my fashion choices, I am hitting the high street. It's time I started wearing T-shirts with writing on them again. My receding hairline? I'm getting a transplant. My body? I'm getting ripped and I'm going to run that marathon. I won't sit down in a comfortable chair and watch my 40s descend into jumpers and elasticated chinos. I'm going to punch my 40s in the balls and become a DILF god. If not, hopefully I'll have a decent BMI score by the end of it …

I wrote down in my diary,

> *'By this time next year, I will be twelve-and-a-half stone. I'll have a three pack (got to be realistic). Be physically fit. Dress better. Find inner happiness. Fly a plane. Be the best husband and father in the country and finally get my hair back.'*

I knew I needed a Plan. I thought about the basics. What were my main areas to fix? I wrote down three: Weight, Fitness, Mind.

My plan for Weight was simple. For years, I had tried best practice, planned long-term goals and lifestyle changes. Now, it was time to change tack. I wrote down: 'Anything that you think will give you quick results.'

Under the heading Fitness, I wrote: 'Run every day, no matter what'.

And under Mind? Well, I didn't know what to write. My mind was empty. I knew I had issues. I knew that I was all over the place mentally, but I didn't know what to write. I left it blank. Firstly, I was going to right the wrongs of my running shambles a decade previously.

I've always been an imperial measurement kind of guy. Even though Ireland has been a member of the EU for nearly fifty years and has used the metric system for the last twenty, I have been mentally colonised by the British Empire when it comes to inches, yards and miles. It's the same with clothes and particularly shoe sizes. I'm never going to ask a sales assistant for a shoe size '43'; it will always be a '9' for me. It's not because I lack the ability to see that the metric system is a better system, or that I'm sadomasochistically whipping myself with the yoke of Empire, it's because I've diagnosed myself with dyscalculia, which is dyslexia with numbers.

I've always been hopeless with maths. When I was younger, I would remember my times tables like a poem. Where most kids would see the numbers $7 \times 2 = 14$, I would learn it off in my head as 'Seven times two equals fourteen'. Try doing long division like that! So, when it comes to understanding measurements, albeit ones as bonkers as the imperial scale, they're the only ones I know now. It is particularly difficult when doing up babies' bottles. Every bottle you buy now is in millimetres, yet I use ounces. When you're nearly falling asleep with a screaming baby in your arms and you're trying to work out what 100ml is in ounces and then trying to remember how many scoops you've already put into the bottle, it's surprising that any of our babies have survived under my care at all. As for land sizes, it drives me bonkers when I hear a news feature on the telly with something like 'this development is over five hundred hectares in size with over 100,000 square metres of commercial property'. They might as well be saying, 'this development is a yellow fluffy banana with over 100,000 purple talking butterflies'. I only understand acres and feet. Needless to say, I will never be employed in real estate.

I never thought I would be that person who actively blocks technological development from my life. When I hear teenagers talking about artists 'dropping' a song on Spotify, I try to pretend I know what they are talking about. Then I have to remind myself that if a person from 1824 were to visit me in a time machine, we could easily talk about my shoe size and how many scoops of baby formula I need on a nightly basis. So, when my wife suggested that I do the 'Couch to 5k', I immediately thought: I'm not some Millennial. I don't run 5ks. And it has always been a 'sofa' not a 'couch'. So, I decided that I would begin my 'sofa to 3.106855961 miles'. Not as catchy, I accept.

The couch-to-5k idea has been around for over a decade and the greasy arms of online shopping have firmly embraced it. When I googled it, I had the option of over fifty apps that would get me from overweight, ginger Irishman to long-distance Olympian Haile Gebrselassie in under a month. Also, the avalanche of ads for running shoes, shorts, chafing waxes, socks, powdered minerals and even altimeters that I was bombarded with made me think that the algorithms Google used are not only intrusive and aggressive, but also utterly useless. If the people who wrote the coding obviously targeting me as a 'runner' called to my house on a Saturday morning and saw me in my underpants trying to control three small children, they would be embarrassed at offering me 'zinc and magnesium hydration powders'. If the Google Analytics team really knew their stuff, they would be calling around to the house offering to babysit every second weekend.

I don't mind Amazon or Google knowing everything about my life. In fact, I find it useful. Without the diary function on my phone, I wouldn't show up anywhere. The fact that Amazon can tell me what toys to buy for my kids' birthdays or that Google Maps follows me everywhere doesn't annoy me: it fills me full of joy when it tells me where I've left my car and not to forget 'your anniversary – here is where you can buy flowers'. In fact, the more online apps that follow me and tell me what to buy and where to go, the better. I have no issue with G.D.P.R. Until a year ago, I thought it was the old name for East Germany. The reason why I don't care is because I'm an extremely forgetful person, who doesn't plan on murdering anyone soon. So, they can listen to my conversations all they want as long as they don't forget my wife's birthday.

But when it was suggested that I buy a pair of 'Nike Vaporfly shoes', it was crossing the Rubicon. I hadn't run for a bus in ten years and I was getting ads suggesting that I buy a pair of Vaporfly running shoes. The shoes have been worn by the first athletes to do a sub-two-hour marathon. I was planning on just over three miles in six weeks. World Athletics, the association that represents amateur athletes, was planning on banning them at one point because they were seen as giving athletes an advantage due to their design and carbon footplate (whatever that is). I googled them and realised that I was a good 25 years too old to think about running a sub-two-hour marathon but then the glitzy online hook reeled me in, with customer quotes like:

> *'These will change your life.'*
> *'I never thought running could be made so easy.'*
> *'Buy them; you won't regret it.'*
> *'Throw money at it, you idiot'* (this one didn't exist).

I had a perfectly good pair of runners in the boot of my car that I had only used once in the last five years, but I clicked on the bright yellow 'buy now' button and sat back and awaited my order confirmation. Then I went the full hog. I just cannot resist when Amazon tells me, 'Customers who ordered this also ordered this … and this.'

Forty-five minutes later I had purchased:

- ☑ Superhuman f##king amazing running shoes €270
- ☑ Hydration backpack €27
- ☑ Running light lamp €22
- ☑ Compression socks €36
- ☑ Running gloves €18
- ☑ Running anti-chafe socks 5 pack €35
- ☑ 2-in-1 gym and running shorts €22
- ☑ Running shorts briefs €24
- ☑ Hi-vis running top €14

- ☑ Men's quick-drying long-sleeve running top €29
- ☑ Anti-chafe stick €19
- ☑ One year's full subscription to running app €40

Total before I'd taken one step: €556

Over the next few days, those Amazonian brown boxes of hope gradually arrived at our door. Each day I would pry open the Kevlar-like black sticky tape and peer into the endless protective bubble wrap, slowly revealing to my brain the little trinkets of fitness nirvana. Then, on day four, the runners arrived. I knew the next few days would mark the start of the new me. Running Bernard. Slim and mindful. I'd be hanging around with socially conscious CEOs within a matter of weeks. If I got the opportunity, I would proudly say in conversation, 'Oh, what do I do to keep fit? I run. Yeah, I'm a runner.'

That night, I packed all the gear into the boot of my car. My plan was to drive to the Phoenix Park, which is near my house, and on my way home from the office every day I would run – hail, rain or shine. Lying in bed, I opened up my new running app. I chose the section marked 'my first 5k'. The app would coach me over the next few weeks with audio cues, while I was running. My virtual coach was a young healthy-looking American woman with teeth designed by Colgate and hair stolen from an oestrogen factory. She told me things like 'You've got this', and, 'By May you'll be running 5k.' I fell in love with her. She didn't judge me or laugh at me. I felt she knew me. She said things like 'Getting outside is hard'. She was so right – it is so hard, especially when there are so many car-review videos to watch on YouTube. I felt like she knew that underneath my flab, there was a seriously fit and sexy guy. She knew that I was sensitive but tough and cried when songs came on the radio that reminded me of my twenties. However, as I have the most Catholic-Irish mind on the planet, even though she was an online coach, I imagined meeting her parents. Her father didn't like me. I imagined he was from upstate New York and secretly didn't like the Irish. I had fallen in love not just with her, but with her mother, too, who was so sweet. Although this was completely made up in my head, within seven to eight minutes of getting into bed I had to break up with her and choose a young man instead who also said, 'You've got this', and 'by May you'll be running 5k'. I'm possibly the only person I know who has to self-sabotage their daydreams.

My wife looked at my phone from across the bed. 'I use that app. It's good … remember, Bernard, you haven't run in years, so take it easy.'

I sighed. 'I really can't see myself having to walk every hundred yards, sure I do that every day.'

She looked at me. 'Don't dislocate your knee again, Bernard, we have three kids now and even though you don't help out enough, I can't be looking after you on crutches as well.'

Eager not to start a fight, I replied, 'Relax, will you, I've run before.'

She wasn't convinced. 'I'm warning you, Bernard, you think you know everything. That app is designed to get people like you back running easily and slowly.'

Undeterred by my wife's encouragement I set a reminder on my phone: 'Run Phoenix Park 15:00.'

I put together all the items I'd bought on Amazon for my maiden run at the end of the week. I drove into the park at 2:30 in the afternoon. I opened up my boot. I stared at the €556 worth of running gear. I'd financially blackmailed myself into doing this.

I put on the €270 running shoes. I noticed that they were incredibly light. It was just a pity that I had to put them on sitting down. I turned on the app on my phone and realised I had nowhere to put it. The shorts had no pockets. Why would a manufacturer make shorts without putting a pocket in them? I remembered the armband holders that kept popping up on Amazon. 'People who bought these running shorts also bought this.' Yeah, they bought it alright because apparently civilisation has moved on so much in the last ten years that it's not *de rigueur* anymore to have feckin' pockets. Now, I had no other option than to just hold my phone while I ran and wait until I got home to spend another tranche of the children's college money on iPhone armbands. In the Greek legend of Marathon, Pheidippides ran 26 miles to Athens to tell the Greeks that they had defeated the Persians. I think if he hadn't dropped dead, he would have definitely ordered a 'water-resistant cellphone armband in matt black for iPhone and Android' the next time he had to deliver such news.

I began to run, and I felt released, like a greyhound out of a trap. I felt my chest burning. The app vibrated and announced, 'Now, walk for two minutes.' I laughed at its lousy efforts to slow me down. How dare some carefully calculated Californian lifestyle app stop me from what I'm naturally engineered to do? My lungs were burning a bit but that was to be expected. Again, those feelings rushed through my body. I felt my heart pound. I felt tears in my eyes from the cold wind. I felt strong.

I felt a stabbing pain in my left knee.

Oh shite. Again, a stabbing pain in my knee. It was the same knee. Two women were running towards me, but I couldn't stop. Call it pride, or more accurately, ego. They should have seen me seven minutes ago. I'd been exactly like them. Now, I was a runner. I was determined not to stop. I got past them and then the mother of all pain jolted through me. It reminded me of the time my sister accidentally stabbed me with a knitting needle on Christmas Day 1987. Now, my brain was screaming, 'Stop, you f**king idiot.' I ran into a little bunch of trees beside a manmade lake that was home to several ducks. I looked down at my knee. It looked OK, but when I went to walk on it, the pain started again. Now, I understood the whole walk-run thing but of course, I'd had to go all in. All I could hear was my wife's voice in my head: 'Take it easy, or you'll hurt yourself.' But the most unusual feeling was emanating from my nipples. They were on fire. I tried to shove my head down the collar of my T-shirt, but it wouldn't fit. I eventually took the shirt off and when the cold air hit them, it felt heavenly. They looked like the starter buttons on ride-along lawnmowers. One of them (the left one) was bleeding. How had this happened after only ten minutes? I touched one of them. Jesus, the pain! It was like my finger was a mini sander. People apparently pay for this type of torture and humiliation.

Forty-five minutes later, I was sitting in the driver's seat. The app spoke: 'Now walk,' and I looked at the screen. I had run 1.2 miles. Just over a mile and I had damaged my knee again and my nipples. Why couldn't I just have followed the instructions? I could hear my wife's voice over and over again in my head. 'You think you know everything.' The problem is I *do* think I know everything. Surely that's what being a confident person is? A person who knows everything ... apart from his physical limitations. I looked down at my knee again. It wasn't dislocated, but it had swollen into a balloon.

When I got back to the house I hobbled into the shower. As the cold water added a nice layer of ice onto my misery, I noticed my body in the mirror. It wasn't me. I was horribly unbalanced in my obesity. My legs, bum and arms were fine, but my stomach was massive. Then I noticed one new extension … moobs. I'd never noticed until now that I was developing breasts. I judged them to be at least AA size and I'm rarely wrong. It was why I'd chafed my nipples – as I was running, I'd been jiggling. Now I understand why women wear sports bras. In fact, how do women run at all? All I could think was, would I need a sports bra? That's one thing I bet Amazon doesn't have, a sports bra for men.

My stomach had developed new geographical features since I'd properly looked at it last. The first thing I noticed was how deep my belly button had become. The layers of fat around it had grown so much that I was harvesting a small bale of belly-button fluff from it daily. I was amazed at how much it was producing. If I were a conceptual artist I might have saved it and made a jumper from it, then saved the fluff that came off that one and made another jumper and so on, until I had twenty or so jumpers made of belly-button fluff. I'd call the exhibition 'Fluffing Me'. Finding a gallery to put that on could prove difficult.

My love handles had branched out as two separate independent countries. Where once they'd protruded like the small hand grabs that hang from the ceiling on a tram, they were now capable of accommodating two medium-sized hamsters on each. What was really shocking was the joining of the top half (my moobs) to the bottom half (my belly). I remembered the term 'conurbation' from my secondary-school geography classes 25 years before. This was where a city would become so big, it would engulf the smaller towns that surrounded it and eventually those towns would become part of one large urban mass. Well, that's exactly what was happening to my upper body. Twenty-five years ago, I'd been slagged for being thin and scrawny. Today I'd struggle to fit into the desk and chair at my old school.

My bum, it seemed, had done the complete opposite. It had retreated into my legs and had started making it way slowly up my back. I was also developing what I call 'belt branding'. There was now a permanent loop of red around my waist. It had developed as my stomach had grown bigger and my belt and grown tighter and tighter until it left marks like a wedding ring. It became a shallow red canal around me. But then there was the scariest sight of all: The Overhang. I'd only ever seen overhangs on old men in saunas – now, I was developing one. An overhang is where the fat on your stomach increases so much it spills out from the torso and 'hangs' over your belt. I now had one.

For years I'd look at my ever-expanding body and always have the same thought: 'That's it. Tomorrow I'm starting a diet and exercise regime.' But it never worked. I've gotten the best advice; I have had one-on-one sessions with dieticians. I've started every fitness fad hundreds of times and always stopped. Now, naked with a swollen knee and bleeding nipples, I had the first realistic thought of my 40s. Was this just me? Is this body, this mind, this person, me? Am I ever going to change? Should I change? Again, I could hear my wife's voice: 'You think you know everything.' Maybe I don't, but I do know me.

I always knew that diet and exercise was the best approach to losing weight and that's the road I always took. I never tried fad diets because I know they just prey on the weak and take their money. But here I was, almost 17 stone, bleeding from the nipples. Why wouldn't I try a few fad diets? Why couldn't I be sold a lie every now and then? I knew that if I slowly started exercising again and beginning to eat better, it would only last about two weeks and I'd be back to my normal ways. So, I decided I didn't need a plan. I needed a quick fix. Just saying it to myself lifted a shroud of anxiety off me. I was being honest with myself for probably the first time in 40 years. I don't have resilience, I'm not patient, I'm not a long-term kind of guy. I'm a hot-tempered, excitable, impatient man – and why not indulge that man?

That night in bed, I planned the second part of my 40th-birthday promise to myself. I'd tackle my weight once and for all. Meanwhile, I knew I had to hide my dud knee from my wife. 'How was your run?' she asked.

I took a second to answer. 'Yeah, grand.'

She replied instantly, 'You're lying … I saw you hobble up the stairs.'

I was about to explain myself when she added, 'I bet you didn't follow the app like it said: walk-run, walk-run. I bet you decided to run quickly and injured yourself and that's why you're limping.'

I have to be right all the time, so I contradicted her. 'No, in fact, I feel great. I'm probably going to run again tomorrow.'

In response, she turned over and breathed the word 'liar'.

I couldn't sleep. My knee was killing me. It was uncomfortable to even have the weight of the duvet on it. I grabbed my phone. I googled 'quick weight-loss diet'. To my horror, I realised that Google was now policing itself. No matter what way I searched – 'lose weight fast', 'quickest diet for weight loss', even 'regardless of my health, tell me how to lose weight quickly' – it kept returning the same results: drink more water, increase your protein intake, cut your carb consumption, start lifting weights, eat more fibre, set a sleep schedule, stay accountable, blah blah blah. I knew all this. What I wanted were some dark-web results. I wanted to see things like 'Eat these four scorpions and you will lose 100lbs in two weeks.' All that kept popping up were pictures of toned American women drinking lemon water in front of sunsets on whitewashed verandas as they proclaimed the virtues of drinking lemon water in the morning.

However, things began to pick up around page 16 of the search results. The first one that really caught my eye was 'The Clay Diet'. It consisted of consuming edible clay along with your regular diet. It provided three important factors that I was looking for. Firstly, you could buy it. Unlike 'moderation' or 'patience', I could get the stuff delivered. Secondly, you took it along with your regular diet. Finally, this clay would fill up my stomach with something that wasn't chocolate. It was, apparently, according to the website, 'a medicine practised for thousands of years in parts of Africa and the Middle East'. The practice of eating clay is called 'geophagia'. I Google 'geophagia' and discover that it was common in pre-industrial societies for pregnant women and children to eat clay so they could get the zinc and iron that was deficient in their diet. I started to wonder about my Guinness habit. I normally drink all the Guinness in Dublin until I fall over when I'm on a night out. Guinness has iron in it. It used to be given to pregnant women in Ireland and to blood donors. HAVE I AN IRON DEFICIENCY? There and then I diagnosed myself. I'm not overweight because I eat the wrong food or don't exercise regularly, it's because I'm mineral deficient!

I went straight onto Amazon and straight into a conundrum. You'd think edible clay was … edible clay. No. There were grey clay chunks for natural eating, superfine food-grade detoxifying clay, Malawi edible kaolin clay chunks, yellow clay chunks, red clay chunks, sapphire clay chunks, bentonite clay. Edible chalk had its own subsection, which included LISIC and Monastic edible chalk chunks. I imagined two middle-aged men meeting up in their favourite clay bar a thousand years ago only to find the menu bamboozling. One would turn to the other and say, 'You just can't get a plain cup of clay anymore.'

I decide on the most-bought package: 'Premium nutri-clay – 250g superfine food-grade internal-use detoxifying clay'. It was also described as 'edible healing clay'. Mmmmm – tasty.

Next, I trawled through Google and the list of diets was endless: keto, intermittent fasting, vegan, Paleo, the South Beach diet and the water diet. But one jumped out at me. A bizarre belief called 'breatharianism'. This was a diet based on just breathing air, eating basically nothing. People who followed this diet were known to have died. As much as it seemed desperate to order edible clay online, there was no way I was going to be putting two slices of nitrogen, oxygen and carbon dioxide in the toaster the following morning. The water diet seemed interesting and I figured that I had loads of that stuff downstairs. The most common trend was to drink 'a gallon a day'. Like the clay, you just had to try and drink a gallon of water every day to lose weight. This looked easy. It worked on the principle of filling your stomach up with non-calorie bulk and God bless the Americans, they still use gallons. The term '3,785 millimetres of water per day' just doesn't have the same ring to it. Next, I downloaded an app to record my intake. The idea was that every time you drank water, you put the amount into the app and a picture of a man filled from his feet up. Who knew water and clay would be the key to my weight loss?

Just as I was about to turn in, I noticed the word 'OMAD' pop up at the bottom of the page. In fact, when I scrolled back through the pages, I kept seeing OMAD again and again. I clicked on a magazine article and there it was: One Meal a Day. It was basically nirvana for me. You eat one meal a day

– as much as you can at one sitting – and that was it. It made perfect sense to me. I never want to eat breakfast. I can't eat in the morning. I eat at night. It's like a switch goes off in my head when the sun goes down. A tiny little person in my head pushes a giant lever and it illuminates a bright red neon light spelling ICE-CREAM. Was this for real, I wondered. Could you actually lose weight by eating just one meal a day? If so, that was the diet for me. All the lectures about weight loss and timing, portion size, exercise and moderation and here's little old non-expert me with the answer: 1) eat clay 2) drink a gallon of water 3) eat one meal a day. If that didn't work, I'd Google 'weight-loss surgery' next.

One issue with my jaunt in the park, apart from me apparently exposing myself, was my knee. I could walk on it but running was now out of the question. I googled 'Can you lose weight from walking?' Again, all I could see were numbers. If I walked 10,000 steps a day, I could lose 3,500 calories a week and 3,500 calories are equal to one pound of body weight. Jesus, I just wanted the quick answer. Exasperated, I tried 'How do you lose weight quicker by walking?' Again, safe, sanitised Google gave me lovely answers based around terms like 'headspace', 'brisk' and the worst of all, 'in conjunction with a balanced diet'.

It was then, lying in bed, I noticed a trend. If you want the crazy stuff on Google, you need to search from page ten on. Eventually all roads led to weighted vests. The idea is that if you carry extra weight, you burn more calories. I picked the coolest looking one on Amazon. There was a picture of a man wearing one who looked like he could kill you if he shook your hand. The vest made him look like he was involved in special forces. It had twenty little pouches on it, each with a 4-oz weight in it.

It was time for maths, a subject that I find not so much difficult as impossible. I calculated that with the vest fully loaded I would be carrying an extra three stone on my usual walk. I then calculated that if I were to walk 10,000 steps with it on me, or roughly five miles, I would burn 1000 calories. I multiplied that by seven and divided it by 3,500 (how many calories in a pound) and bingo, two pounds a week.

On top of the clay, the water and one meal a day, I calculated I would lose four pounds a week. That would be 16 pounds a month.

Thus, by my calculations I would weigh 12-and-a-half stone by 29 July 2019. I picked up my diary and wrote it down on the page for that day:

Diary entry 29 July 2019
Weigh-in day – you will be twelve-and-a-half stone.

I felt weirdly calm. Then I began to feel anxious because I felt calm. I hadn't felt good about myself for so long, I'd forgotten how it felt. I was making headway in spite of myself. I had my diet sorted (well, I'd wait until the clay arrived). Then I remembered my nipples. I wondered if you could get a sports bra for men. The answer … yes. Except they are called 'chest protectors' or, 'GPS-tracking chest supports'. They are basically bras for men. One final click and a further €34 spent. A week into my plan, I had spent €617, couldn't walk properly and had bleeding nipples but at least there were more brown boxes of hope on the way – and I still had a plan, of sorts. I finally turned over and tried to sleep.

Next, I needed to work on my mental health, especially my anxiety. I've always been an anxious person. The problem for anxious people is that there is so much talk about being anxious in the media now that it actually makes us anxious. Here's how my anxiety works for me:

I'll think about buying a new car. Then I'll think about the cost. Then I'll think about the person selling it to me. I'll tell them I can't afford it, then they will say, 'Well, why are you wasting my time?' I'll have no answer and to apologise, I'll buy the car on credit. Then I'll have to find the money each month to pay for the car. Then I'll start thinking my family is going to go hungry while a new car sits in my driveway and we can't even eat. I'll go back to the man who sold it to me, and he will buy it back off me for half the price. He'll then tell everybody he knows that my family is starving and I've given him back the car. I'll be a laughingstock. My pride will be hurt, my family starving and my wife will be on the phone talking to her friends, crying her heart out. It will end up on social media and my mother will call me, crying as well. I'll eventually have to move out of the house because I can't be trusted with the kids' wellbeing anymore. I'm picturing living rough beside a train station and eventually I contract rabies. Twenty seconds ago, I was just THINKING about buying a car – now I'm a rabid destitute.

So, when I Google my thoughts and behaviour, the one word that keeps popping up is Mindfulness. I've always had a deep mistrust of Mindfulness. The word itself has always felt sinister to me. If you take phrases like 'free love', 'life is for living' or '*carpe diem*', they have been ground out of thousands of years of experience. I know they are true even if they are regularly shoved onto advertisements for soft drinks or credit cards. Yet the very concept of Mindfulness makes me think of an industry. It reminds me of homoeopathy. As much as well-meaning people swear by its benefits, I just can't stop the little man in my brain screaming, 'IT'S WATER'. The same little man screams, 'It's MASS', every time I hear Mindfulness. When I hear people talking about 'being in the present', 'switching off your mind', 'staying away from technology' and my favourite, 'allowing yourself to be bored', all I can think of is Mass.

When I was a child, my mother and father would make us go to Mass. I remember thinking on Sundays, Oh no, not again. I used to wonder if all the other kids in the world thought the same of their religious practices. At Mass, we would sit in the same seat every Sunday. Myself and my sisters would be bored to tears. Luckily, there would always be something that would entertain us, the same things that would happen at every Mass in the country. I used to call them the 3FCs. The first F was a fart. You could always rely on someone farting in Mass. It would normally eke itself out at the quietest of moments, nearly always when the priest was saying, 'Now, let's be silent and think of people who have gone to the Kingdom of Heaven'. Heads would bow and stillness would settle gently on the congregation. And then, like a gift, someone would produce a whopper of a fart. It would echo and bounce off every wall. The beauty was that if you laughed, my father would go berserk. You couldn't laugh in Mass, so it gave us all the more pleasure as we tried our best not to.

The second F would be a fall. There is a well-worn phrase in Ireland: 'They took a bad fall outside Mass.' It's often the first domino in the demise of an elderly person. I remember once falling on my way back from Communion and hitting my head off a collection plate. When I returned to my seat, my sisters were laughing so hard their eyes had turned red.

And finally, the final F, which is actually a C. There was always a small child who'd nonchalantly make its way up onto the altar and start to pull on the priest's vestments or try to grab the chalice. They always made for great entertainment.

However, the main point of Mass was to be quiet for an hour once a week and when you're twelve years of age, this is near impossible. Generally, I've no problem with religion. I completely understand those who believe. I've wandered along in life without any real faith as such. I was brought up a Catholic and when I was a young child, I was obsessed with religion. I wore rosary beads, knew all the prayers and was convinced the picture of the Sacred Heart in our kitchen was moving. Over time, my zealous behaviour decreased. Puberty gave me an 'everything's shite' mindset and by the time I got to college, I hadn't much time for the big man or woman in the sky. It was only when I got a bit older and started going to weddings and funerals that I realised, 'Oh, yeah, I remember this place'.

We attended a wedding once with Olivia, our eldest, who was four at the time. It was to be held in a Catholic church and, as she walked around the church, she suddenly asked me, 'Daddy, what are those little houses?' She was pointing at the confession boxes. How do you describe confession to a four-year-old?

Me: They are confession boxes.

Olivia: Like the Santa boxes.

Me: No, they are selection boxes. These are confession boxes. You go in there and tell the priest your sins and Holy God in the sky forgives you.

Olivia: What are sins – are they like bad things?

Me: Yeah.

Olivia: Like what?

Me: Like bad language or … remember when you hit Tadhg over the head with your Our Generation doll … that kind of stuff.

Olivia: But I said sorry to him.

Me: Oh, yeah, I know.

Olivia: So, do I have to say sorry to Holy God? I didn't hit him!

Me: No, you're not saying sorry, you're just …

I was going to try and explain absolution to her but thought that this might be a better tack …

Me: It's just a way of getting it off your mind … sort of.

Olivia: So, I didn't have to say sorry to Tadhg. I could have just gone into the box?

Me: No, you always have to say sorry.

Olivia: In the box as well.

Me: You don't have to but it's … just letting your…

I actually began to struggle now, this being the first-ever meaningful question asked by one of my children.

She looked at me, wrinkled her nose and gave me the answer:

Olivia: Are they magic boxes?

Me: Yes. Yes, well done, they are magic boxes.

Olivia: Can I go in?

Me: No, not yet, you have to wait until you're older and you'll make your First Confession.

Olivia: When I'm seven? You say I can do everything when I'm seven.

Me: Do I?

Olivia: Yeah, you do. You said I could walk to school without holding your hand when I'm seven. You said I can sleep in my own room when I'm seven. Seven is ages away.

Me: Well, you can.

Olivia: I'd better be allowed, Mister.

Here's the thing: as I've said, I'm not good with numbers in any capacity. I struggle with simple maths, with time and especially with dates. So, if I were asked what age children are in first class, my honest answer would be, 'I don't know'. But now that I'm a parent, I'm supposed to know about my children's milestones and when they achieve them. I'm completely on board when kids equate age with height, like when Tadhg says, 'Daddy, when I'm as tall as you, will I be able to drive a train?'

I have no idea what age I was when I made my First Confession. All I remember is that I thought it was odd that I had to make up a sin to tell the priest, just so I had a sin to tell. I could not square that circle.

I remember the priest asking me, 'What are your sins?'

I told him: 'I hit my sister Cáit and I said a bad word.'

Then he said, 'And are you sorry?'

I couldn't do it. I actually couldn't do it. I told him, 'I made up one of those sins to tell you, so I'd have a sin, so that's my sin.' I remember looking at him and he laughed, then he shook his head, trying to swallow his laugh. He breathed out a reply: 'Just say a Hail Mary … In the Name of the Father and …'

And then instead of walking away, I told him, 'I hit Cáit because she hit me first. I wouldn't have hit her if …'

He stopped me. 'It's OK, don't worry about it.'

Again, I couldn't let it slip. 'Do I still have to say the Hail Mary for making up a sin, because I was told we had to have two sins, so I wouldn't have made it up if we only had one sin to tell?'

He looked at me and said something that I still laugh at (I have no idea how many years later). 'If you could, Bernard, that would be great.'

Thus, Ireland is possibly the only country in the world that trains an awful lot of its people to lie. Even though they are harmless lies, nevertheless, it adds a certain flamboyance to everyday smalltalk. I'm not sure, though, if I had done anything bad when I was seven years of age and I'm also pretty sure that most seven-year-olds have nothing to repent. I like most religious ceremonies and enjoy the social gatherings and the sense of community, but confession, I just can't get on board with.

I once had a two-hour-long conversation with a priest about it on the Dublin-to-Belfast train. He was in the self-absolution corner. He said something that nearly got me over the line: 'Confession is about forgiving yourself.' But the only metaphor that goes any way to stop the mental itching for me is Olivia's 'Magic Box' theory. If it works for her, it works for me.

Nonetheless, that nagging theory of mine – that Mindfulness was nothing more than Mass repackaged – wouldn't stop knocking at the back door of my brain. I needed to test the theory.

I rent an office on the south side of Dublin city. Every day, after dropping the kids to crèche and school, I take the train in. The one thing that I've noticed on my journey is the abundance of churches in Dublin. I counted almost fifty spires on an inward journey one day. The other thing that surprises me about Dublin, and I'm sure about many cities, is the amount of hidden churches there are, some of which aren't actually all that hidden. I've walked past humongous giants of stone every day for years and haven't realised that they were houses of prayer. Once, while I was in my office, I googled 'churches near me'. The city is literally riddled with them. The old joke about Starbucks – that there is one nearly every hundred metres in any city in the world and in between is another Starbucks – rings true. Churches and pubs are to Dublin what coffee houses are to Seattle.

Eventually, I picked a church that was around the corner from my office. It was so long since I'd been at Mass that I'd actually forgotten that it has a start time. I'd drifted into a space-time continuum for a while that envisioned a priest saying Mass 24 hours a day, just for me. So, I had to wait until the scheduled time.

The bizarre thing is that once I decided to go to the Mass, I started to remember the rules. The first one that came back was fasting. Knowing that my weight-loss journey was definitely going to begin on the following Monday I was a culinary *tour de force* and very much enjoying myself. I was having a bun after my dinner every day and getting an ice-cream for the train ride home. In fact, I was eating so much ice-cream that the kids had noticed. One evening Olivia asked me what I was eating. I knew she wouldn't like to hear that it was rum and raisin ice-cream, so I slightly bent the truth and told her it was custard.

She later told Lorna, 'Mum, I know why Daddy has such a big belly.'

'Oh, why?' Lorna asked.

'Because when I come down here in the morning, I see empty tubs of custard.' Later that week, Olivia informed me very solemnly during bedtime stories: 'Daddy, if you keep eating tubs of custard, your belly will explode.' The reason I mention this is because I felt the same guilt about food when Olivia asked me to stop eating custard as I had done as a child when I'd eaten sweets during Lent.

A teacher once said to us when we were in First Class in primary school: 'If Jesus could go into the desert for forty days and forty nights surely ye can give up smokey-bacon crisps.'

I innocently raised my hand and asked the teacher, 'Did they have smokey-bacon flavour millions of years ago?' I was way too young to understand that Jesus wouldn't have eaten bacon, and thus giving up the crisps would have been the equivalent of six-year-old me giving up alcohol.

Now, 34 years later, I was checking my watch to see if I'd fasted for a full hour before going to Mass. I knew that, in order to receive Holy Communion, you had to fast for an hour beforehand but why, I didn't know. I was about to Google it and I stopped. I stopped because I'd set myself a challenge to see if going back to Mass would help with my anxiety and make me, dare I say it, more mindful. It wasn't a fact-finding mission.

Four minutes later, I googled it. Canon law states that fasting is to enable a cleansing of the soul to prepare for taking Christ. I then went onto my calorie app. If I were to fast every hour before Mass at 1 pm, that would mean I could eat my one meal a day an hour later at 2 pm when I got out. My mindful voyage was already helping me to lose weight. Then I had a brainwave. What if I was to get my exercise in too? I worked out that there was a church exactly 2.5 miles from my office. I'd walk there with my weighted vest on, take in a Mass at 1 pm, walk back, dump the vest, then eat my one meal a day. Now, I had a real plan. I wrote it out that night on a big sheet of paper:

Daily Weight-loss, Fitness and Mindfulness Plan for the Next Two Weeks

6:30 am: *wake, drink one pint water, do crèche drop-off, school run*
9:30 am: *take the train into work, drink one pint of water on train.*

10:15: *walk to office. Work until twelve noon.*
12 noon: *drink one pint water. Walk to Mass wearing weighted vest.*
1 pm: *Mass.*
2 pm: *walk back to office. Drink one pint water.*
2:30 pm: *eat edible clay, followed by the permitted one meal a day.*
3 pm: *drink one pint of water.*
4:30 pm: *walk to train.*
5:15 pm: *pick up kids. Drink one pint of water.*
6:30 pm: *drink one pint of water.*
7:30 pm: *put kids to bed.*
8:30 pm: *drink one pint of water.*
9:00 pm: *bed.*

At the end, I wrote, *'Remember, don't be a Belgian Koala.'* *

(*Once, in my twenties, I was in Belgium seeing a friend, when an Australian barmaid shared an interesting observation about koalas. The story begins with me boarding the wrong train. I had no ticket and I got caught. I lied to a train inspector and got kicked off the train. So, I had to spend the night in Antwerp, which I decided to spend sleeping outside an Irish bar. At closing time, I was desperate to have another drink. I got talking to the barmaid about Australia and then the subject moved onto koala bears. She told me she had worked on a koala reserve and said that they are asocial. They will have some interactions but just won't or can't adapt to different surroundings. Then she said something that has stuck with me: 'They sleep half the day and even though they do very little except eat, when they are awake, they get bored really easily.' That's me. I've actually coined the phrase 'koala culture' to describe myself, because at times it seems like I feel bored from being bored, even though I've always work to get through. I'm a massively overweight koala bear. So, every now and again I say to myself: 'Don't be a Belgian koala today'.)

At last, the great day came. A full three months after my 40th birthday, I was determined to snap back into my youthful shape. I checked my homespun maths again. It looked right. It was right. No more thinking, just doing. Tomorrow was D Day. Dad Day, a day when I'd invent the quick elixir of youth for men in their 40s everywhere. I imagined being interviewed on TV chat shows about how I came up with the method. I was going to save myself and thousands, no, millions of other men from their mid-life crises. The date of 15 April 2019 would go down in history as the day the belly bulges, receding hairlines and beige apocalypse ended. It was finally time to put my Weight, Fitness and Mindfulness plan into action. I had bought the clay, the weighted vest, and had planned a strenuous route to work that would guarantee that I'd reach my step count for the day.

Here's what happened:

06:30 a.m.

I wake to Seán kicking me in the head. I had to bring him into the bed during the night as he wouldn't settle. I think I might get an extra minute and that he'll nod off again. Lorna has already gone to work so there is space for him in the bed, but he persists. Eventually he starts jumping on my head like it is a rodeo bull in a student bar during rag week. Olivia and Tadhg start shouting from the bottom of the stairs, 'Dad, we want our breakfast now.' I get the kids their breakfasts and give Seán his bottle. Next up is a pint of water for me. I fill it from the tap and drink it in about four gulps. I didn't realise how easy it is going to be. Everyone online and in the real world is harping on about how difficult it will be, but they are wrong.

06:45

The kids aren't dressed yet. I've gone to the toilet twice already.

07:00

I am now begging Tadhg to put his shoes on. Olivia can't find her favourite bow for her hair and she tells me that she can't go in without it as she was going to show it to her teacher. Seán has found my bag of clay and is trying to bite into the end of it. Tadhg now is trying his level best to do a headstand.

07:30

I've had to hoover twice, fashion two hair bows together and give Seán another bottle, but we're in the car. I have a bottle of water with me that I'll have to drink on the drive. It holds just under a pint.

07:33

I've drunk half the bottle of water. The kids are fighting over what song they want played in the car. Olivia wants 'Let it Go', Tadhg wants 'Baby Shark'. They could not have chosen two more inappropriate songs as my bladder is quite literally about to burst. I'm thinking I might have to get out of the car and go for a wee.

07:40

We get to the door of the crèche. I ask if I can I use their toilet. The relief. Olivia gets back in the car with me. I'll stay with her until I drop her off at school at nine. 'Dad,' she says, 'Why are you going to the toilet so much?' That's a very good question – why am I? Undeterred, I drink the rest of the pint.

08:00

We're back home. I barely make it to the toilet. This can't be right? I've only drunk two pints and I've gone for a number one four times. I think to myself that maybe my body was so desperate for water before now that it has no idea what it is and has to try to get rid of it. Nonetheless, I fill another pint glass. I get it down me. The only bonus is I'm not hungry. Three pints of water down already.

08:30

Myself and Olivia start walking to school. I don't feel the need to 'go', thank God. Before we left the house, she asked me, 'Do you need to go, Dad, because there are only kids' toilets in my school?' It reminded me of my parents drilling their mantra into us on every trip that we took: 'Go now, because we're not stopping.'

'I'm fine, Olivia,' I assured her.

08:32

I'm bursting. We have to go back to the house. Olivia says, 'I told you to go before we left.'

08:40

We start our walk to school for the second time.

08:50

We're standing in the playground. I feel the urge to go again. I can't believe this is happening. I begin to get fidgety. Olivia notices. 'Dad, don't you dare go to the toilet in the kids' toilets … Do you hear me, Mister?' I start to plead with all of the gods to open up the school.

09:00

The doors open and the teachers come out. I kiss Olivia goodbye and bolt for home. I hear another parent shout at me, 'Bernard, her bag!' In my haste, I was running away with Olivia's schoolbag. Oh, Christ, I've to double back. I give it to her. She stares at me: 'You're not going here, Mister.'

I run out onto the main road. This time it's serious – I actually feel like I'm going to piss my pants. I keep telling my brain to stop. It knows I'm ten minutes away from my house, too far to hang on, so it's telling my bladder to release. I do a deal with my brain: you stop telling my bladder we're doomed, and I'll stop whacking my head off low door frames.

09:07

I get back to the house. I can't help but think I've also got a seven-minute jog in. Will I count that towards my calorie burn today? I get to the toilet – just about.

09:10

This has to stop. I've only had three pints of water and already I've almost wet myself more frequently than Seán. I look at one of his nappies and think, should I stuff one down the front of my underpants? This is crazy. I need a strategy to deal with my spending pennies. I drink another half-pint and wait.

09:30

I go again. Fifth time today. I calculate that for every half-pint

I drink, I need to go half an hour later. For every pint I drink, I need to go 15–20 minutes later. Half pints from now on.

09:40

I load the car with my weighted vest and a bag containing my edible soil. I drive to the park near my house and pull up just across from the President of Ireland's residence. I look at the Tricolour fluttering in the wind, being gently spat at by the constant Irish drizzle. It seemed to be telling me, 'Come on, Bernard, today is the first day of President O'Shea's attack on his flab.' I put on the vest with patriotic pride and realise I have a problem. The plan was to wear the vest as I walked the four miles to and from my office, while also picking up an extra two miles going to Mass, resulting in a total of ten miles. However, the vest is massive, and I can't get my rain jacket over it. I catch my reflection in the car window. I look like an overweight US Marine wearing a bulletproof vest. I can't walk into the city centre wearing it – I'll either be arrested or be asked to arrest someone else. I search around in the boot of my car to see if I can find something that will cover it and me. I really notice the weight of the vest then, as I bend over the boot, like a giraffe with a bowling ball on its head. I have definitely forgotten what two stone feels like. It squeezes against my ribs, too, and for a few seconds, I can't breathe. I eventually find a bright pink poncho that my wife bought at a music festival a few months ago. I open it out and thankfully it is big enough to fit over the vest. The only drawback is that on the front of it is written 'THIS IS MY DANCING PONCHO.' I have two choices: look like a person who refuses to let the festival season go, or the person who arrests drug dealers at a festival, so I opt for the former. I salute the flag and begin the four-mile walk into the city centre wearing two stone of lead weights, a bright pink rain poncho and, hopefully, an empty bladder.

11:04

One hour and 24 minutes later, I arrive at my desk. I take off the pink poncho and then the weighted vest. I am not wet from the rain, but my body is soaked with sweat. It has dripped down my back onto my legs. It's lucky that I don't have any meetings on today, but I have to figure out how to deal with the sweat. I don't once think about showering. I feel exhausted but good. I did get a few odd looks with my poncho on, but I did the walk in decent time considering the weight. I am starving but, unbelievably, thirsty!

11:15

I drink another pint of water. That's four pints down. Half-way there on the water and just under half-way on the step count. Feeling proud of myself, I start to work through some emails.

11:16

I am hungry. Really hungry. I feel a bit weak too. I can't eat before I go to Mass because it will be too early. So, I decide to have the edible soil. I get a glass of water and open the sachet. To my dismay, inside it is soil. It looks like soil. It smells like soil. It has the texture of soil. It is soil. I have somehow romantically convinced myself that it is going to be a wholesome, glorious superfood that will taste like the nectar running off a hummingbird's beak. I get a plastic fork and start to whizz it around the glass, but after about fifteen seconds, it sinks to the bottom again. I sniff it – it smells like the steam coming out of the Wellington boots of thousands of mucky concertgoers in a packed tent. I try not to think about its impending taste, and I wolf it down. My initial reaction is to get sick. I try holding it down, but I keep dry retching. Eventually, after another half-pint of water, I force it to settle in my stomach. It is the most unpleasant thing I have ever tasted. I then realise I will be doing this every day for the next two weeks.

12:00

It's an hour before I go to Mass again for the first time in nearly 25 years. I've been to weddings and funerals, but I'd never decided to go to Mass otherwise. I start to think about the vest again. Should I take it off in Mass or leave it on? If I leave it on, I'll have to leave on the pink poncho too.

12:20

Five pints of water down and I've gone to the toilet again. Things are looking up, though, as I know I won't need to go on my walk to the church or my walk back.

12:30

After answering two emails and watching several YouTube videos of how to build a log cabin in the wild, I set off on my Pauline conversion. I walk along St Stephen's Green and watch as people eat their lunch on the lawns. I am wearing the pink poncho and vest and typically, the weather has brightened up considerably, so I'm beginning to bake. I am getting some odd glances but pretend I can't see them. The church I am going to isn't far away, so I pick up the pace.

I arrive at the entrance to the church. It's like so many urban churches in that it's only when you look up that you see the scale of it. This one has double steeples and a large Notre

Dame-style circular stained-glass window in the middle. It is, compared to country churches, a beast. I walk into the lobby. I know it's not called a 'lobby', but I can't think what it is called. I see some people dipping their fingers in a black-marble holy water fountain on their way in. I am not ready for that level of Catholicism yet, so I demur. I walk through the 'holy lobby' and look at the noticeboard. It is cluttered with Mass timetables and ecclesiastical information about sacraments like 'Benediction' and 'the Stations of The Cross' that I haven't thought about since I was an altar boy. I walk through two giant wooden doors with painted handles and am greeted by a smell, just like that of a pub on a busy Friday, or your first coffee in the morning. The smell of a church is very particular, a mix of damp, incense and guilt. Every church smells the same. It's almost like they spray an aerosol (or aerosoul) into the blessed air every day.

I sit at the back. I know I've forgotten when to stand, sit or kneel, so I need to keep a safe distance from the professional Mass-goers, of whom there are only about twenty-five or thirty. The priest walks out onto the altar on his own. He is about seventy years of age and is completely bald with thick-rimmed brown glasses. He has a slight hump on his back, and you can see, even from where I am sitting, that he needs to groom his nose and ear hair. He is still putting the finishing touches to dressing himself, because he is tugging at his vestments trying to get them over his black trousers. He does it just as he reaches the microphone on the altar.

'In the name of the Father, and the Son and the Holy Spirit. You are very welcome here today on the feast of Saint Paternus, whose father was a bishop in Ireland. Paternus didn't follow him, though, he spent his life in Wales. Just goes to show even saints make mistakes.'

The thirty or so people start laughing. I am floored. The guy has opened with a joke! Then he proceeds to – even to this renewed novice – 'fly through it', as they say down the country. As he goes through the motions, I decide to try and get mentally involved in the service. I've always found trying to understand the readings difficult. They are always about somebody visiting somebody's house with news that's really bad, like plagues or an ensuing Roman invasion. They always have names like Zacharia or Hosea and they are always 'letters from St Paul to the Romans.' I used to think, what if St Paul comes back and says, 'Hey, they are my private letters'? But more importantly, how do you send letters to an entire empire without a specific address on them? Could any Roman have opened them?

I listen and try to engage with what the priest is saying, but my mind keeps wandering. I notice a lady to my right about twenty feet away from me constantly glaring over at me. I am wearing the bright pink poncho, so fair enough, but I think she wants to make eye contact, so I am fixated on staring straight ahead. The priest starts the Creed: 'I believe in one God, the Father Almighty, Creator of Heaven and earth, and in Jesus Christ, his only son, our Lord…' And then the second wave of memory hits me. The sound of the mumbling parishioners speaking along with the priest is like a swarm of bees that are trying to remember where they left their house keys. 'Mmmmmm hummm hu huh mmmm mmmmm. Heeee mmmmm.'

I start to feel really pissed off. I came here to get some divine insight into being mindful and all I'm getting are memories of being bored out of my head, praying, ironically enough, for the Mass to end. I look around and most people are just going through the motions. I want it to be insightful. I want internally to praise the other thirty people for coming there every day. I want to look at the priest and think about his theological capacity to heal those with anxiety or fear. But all I am getting are the sounds and smells of absolute complete and utter boredom.

But who am I to expect more? I know I'm selfish to expect this to be the beginning of a new mindful me. Or even to expect it to give me any form of guidance, which it didn't. It makes me think that maybe beneath my memories isn't enlightenment, but simply repetition. Now I feel selfish, stupid and hungry.

The priest quickly clears his throat. 'Let us all take a moment to remember those who have passed.' Ironically, I don't remember this part. It's a nice idea. I start thinking about friends who have passed away. Then, seeping through my brain, comes the oddest of memories. When I was really young, about five or six, I went to a funeral. It was possibly a grandaunt's. I remember putting my foot in a lump of green moss in the graveyard and it was spongy and soft. I looked up and there was a man in a grey Crombie coat wearing a green-and-grey-threaded trilby hat. 'The grass here is so soft,' I said to him. He smiled and was just about to reply to me when …

'May they rest in peace.' The priest has interrupted a memory from the vault of my mind that I can't get back now. He has broken my stream of consciousness. I feel like shouting up, 'Do it again. Tell us to take a moment for those who have passed.' I am now very hungry and furious with the priest because the memories were keeping my hunger at bay.

By the time I have reconciled all my internal issues, we have reached the Consecration of the Eucharist. This is the bit of the Mass that always seems to me like the heavy-metal part. I notice how everybody's behaviour changes, almost as if we are getting to the real deal. 'Lamb of God, you take away the sins of the world ...' Again, I always think of a little sheep walking around forgiving people. Then the 'bong' follows. I just hang my head as steadily as I can, like a Formula 1 driver experiencing extreme G-force, because I notice the same woman now staring at me across the brown waxed benches. I don't go up for Communion. I just want to sample my re-entry into Mass and vaguely feel that receiving Communion would not be fair to those who really believe.

I hate that question: 'Do you believe in God?' That and 'Do you believe in love at first sight?' are constantly hovering around our conversational universe. Nobody ever asks you, 'Do you believe in car parks?' If there were no car parks, there would be a lot fewer cars. If there were no churches, there probably would be a lot fewer Catholics. Car parks and churches exist. It's not an answer, but it works for me.

After Communion, the priest cleared his throat again, took a sharp breath in and said, 'You may now go in peace to love and serve the Lord.' I think George Lucas owes the Catholic Church for that one. I start to shuffle along the brown bench to make my exit. I've always thought that's how they keep them so clean: they let people's buttocks shine the seats as they exit.

Out of the corner of my eye. I see the woman who has been looking over at me, hurriedly trying to block my exit. 'Hello,' she says, 'I don't want to bother you now, I just wanted to ask you ...'

I am expecting, '... Where did you get your poncho?' Or possibly, 'Could you tell me why you seem to be wearing a bulletproof vest?'

Instead, she says, 'Why are you here?'

'Sorry?'

'Why are you here?' she repeats.

'I'm at Mass.'

'I know that, but why are you here?'

'To go to Mass.'

'Is this a skit?' she says. A skit was a word my father would use for any form of comedic sketch. I hadn't heard that word in years.

'Why would I be doing a skit?' I ask her.

'You're on the telly, aren't you?'

'I am sometimes, yeah,' I admit.

'And is this one of your skits?'

'No.'

She looks at me sternly. 'Are you filming this?'

I understand that people are very protective of their faith. I understand that they can be nervous of strangers. I even understand that people might not like you and might make quick assumptions about who or what you are. I get all that. But what I can't understand is that, in spite of the complete lack of a TV crew around me, she thinks that I might be filming myself.

'No, why would I be filming this?'

'For your skit.'

'I'm not doing a skit,' I tell her again.

'So, you're not filming this.' She eyes me suspiciously.

'No. I'm here for the same reason as you are here.'

'Well…' she pauses and bends her head to the side … I'm here to pray.'

I don't know what else to say to her. I have explained to her that I wasn't filming a skit. Is it worth the time and energy to tell her that this is an experiment in Mindfulness and that I thought Mass was going to re-ignite some spiritual momentum in me, or give me clarity on how to calm down, even possibly reduce my waistline?

I go for the second option: 'I'm here because … I'm here.'

She beams. 'Ah, very good. I thought it was a skit.'

She eventually walks away like some kind of spiritual sheriff, making sure I wasn't going to cause some 'kinda skit' in town.

I muster up the energy to get up and make my way out onto the street. I notice the sheriff again inside the porch, picking up leaves that have been temporarily paragliding in the draught. She bundles them back together and presses them into her hands, as if she is going to throw a fireball. We exchange one more glance as I leave. I smile and nod. She just takes a shallow breath in, looks at me in a way that says, 'I don't want to see your type around here anymore,' and scuttles away through another door that I hadn't noticed was there. She then fires the leaves into a bin that is concealed behind a big, brown shutter. Even God hides the bins. It's obvious to me now that she is the caretaker as well as the spiritual sheriff.

13:10

I walk down as far as the corner of Dame Street and South Great George's Street in the city centre, a busy spot, crammed with people and cars. I'm not thinking about the Mass – I'm starving and wonder if I will make it back to the office before I need to pee. I walk in the direction of St Stephen's Green and decide that I'll cut through the park today because I am still below my step count for the day. I watch flocks of Spanish students fling tiny freckles of Brennan's bread at the ducks and I can't help but think, if one of them were to look away,

I'd happily eat it. I head towards a regular lunchtime haunt, a takeaway sushi place that serves hot food.

13:40

At the takeaway, there is only one person in front of me in the queue, so I think, this'll be quick. I know what I want. But unfortunately for me, the person in front of me doesn't. He stands there looking at the board and at the hotplates – actually looking at everything the tiny shop has to offer – and says, 'I don't know what I want'. Then he says, 'What's the sweet-and-sour duck like?' Then he changes his mind. 'Could I get the chicken special without the rice and with noodles instead?'

I'm not a patient person. I think that when there is someone like this in front of you in a queue, you should be allowed take their name and three penalty points should be put on their driving licence. How can you stand in a queue and not know what you want when you get to the top of it? He doesn't even have the capacity to turn to me and let me go ahead. I am seriously starving, and I know that this is going to be my one and only meal of the day. I decide to give him 60 seconds. I start to count backwards – 59, 58 … and then he says, 'Actually, I'll leave it. Thanks anyway,' then he walks out of the shop. I feel like following him for the rest of his life to see if he can actually make a decision about anything. On his wedding day, when he is asked, 'Do you take this person to be your lawfully wedded partner?' he would probably answer, 'I'm not sure – what else do you have?'

I don't even let the person behind the counter ask me what I want. 'A large Singapore noodle and a large duck curry, both with boiled rice please.' This was, I calculated, 1,800 calories. That's what it says on the lunch board anyway. As somebody who has reached the time in his life where eating a meal on your own is the equivalent of a Mardi Gras, it's nice to be constantly reminded of the calorie content of your food. Nothing like a nice sprinkling of guilt on your chips. 'I'll need a fork please,' I add. Normally, I take chopsticks, purely to impress complete strangers with the fact that I can use them. I can't. I know that today I need a fork to shovel the fuel straight into the furnace. The woman behind the counter hands me my two bags and with what strength I have left, I head back to my office to gorge myself.

14:07

I've been wearing the vest all this time, so I walk up the stairs and take off the pink poncho and start ripping the Velcro off the weighted vest. The sweat is dripping off me and I notice that I have bright red streaks all over my shoulders. Luckily, this is a solo lunch, because if I was meeting anybody, the first question they would probably ask me is, 'So, why did the captain of your pirate ship give you a lashing?' I start to wolf down the duck first. I can't get it down my gullet quick enough. Then I start on the noodles.

14:20

I am completely bloated and feel like I am going to have a heart attack. I burp and even though it was consumed hours ago, all I can taste is the edible soil. I feel sick. My shoulder is now killing me. I lie down on the floor. I start to convince myself again. 'In three months' time, I'll be twelve-and-a-half stone.' Then I start to feel a shuddering pain down the left side of my chest. I grab my newly formed left breast. The pain is bad and is moving down towards my leg. I start to panic. I pull my phone out of my pocket. I know it's a heart attack. I have all the symptoms. I try to stand up when an enormous 'Burrrrrrrrpppppppppp-ahhhhhhhhhh' comes out of my mouth. I have all the symptoms of heartburn.

14:22
Relieved I'm not having a heart attack, I get up off the floor and sit down. I am less than half-way through my first day. I look at the plan again. I have two more pints of water to drink and ten thousand more steps to walk with the vest on. I also have the massive interference of work and a deadline.

15:45
I put the vest back on again. It is now breaking the skin on my left shoulder. I look at the pint glass of water on my office table. Without thinking, I just swallow it down.

15:46
I can taste the edible soil again.

15:50
I have just started the walk back to my car in the Phoenix Park when the heavens open. Luckily for me, I am wearing my pink poncho.

15:52
It is teeming down so heavily that the weighted vest is waterlogged. I pass a newsagent on Baggot Street and I can see they are selling cheap brollies.

15:55
I'm in a queue again. At least this one is moving. Of the five or six people in it, two of us are buying a brolly.

15:57

The queue hasn't moved. There is a woman at the counter and whatever her problem is, there are two staff trying to figure it out.

15:59

Through the Chinese whispers that have filtered along the queue, I learn that she is trying to get money taken off her transit card and reimbursed back into her bank account.

16:00

Crisis averted. The transaction is done and there is only one person ahead of me. And then it happens. My bladder screams into the flooded canyon, 'Empty me'. I start to look around to see if there's any sign of a toilet. Then I spot it, beside a little coffee stall, a door with a sign on it that says, 'TOILETS FOR CUSTOMER USE ONLY.' I am a customer. I am going to be one of those 'only' people very soon.

16:01

I hand the young woman the brolly. She tries to scan the barcode but it won't do the 'bip' sound. She has to call over her co-worker.

16:02

Now I am one of those people who needs two people to serve them. If I were behind me in a queue, I would be cursing myself right now.

16:03

She starts to painstakingly enter each digit of the barcode into the till. As she punches each number onto the keypad of the register, she might as well be kicking me in my large intestine. I can't hold it. It feels as if it's coming. I start to think of anything non-water related. That is difficult when it's pissing rain.

16:03:35

'Can I use your toilet please … I'll leave you the card and I'll collect the brolly,' I say.

'Sure – the code is 1998,' she replies.

16:03:55

The code on the door isn't working. I type it in again. 1-9-9-8. I am trying to think of anything to stop myself from peeing myself. 1998: the year France won the World Cup. 1998: my second year in college. 1998 …

It works. I push in the door.

16:04

My brain sees the toilet. I know it does because it wants to tell my bladder to release its contents. I rip off the poncho, then as I am trying to take off the weighted vest, it happens. I am flung back into being a toddler at school. The kid with the weak bladder, running around the playground not wanting to go to the toilet in case I missed anything. As a child, urine played an all-too-large part in my identity. One of my earliest memories is of a teacher laying newspaper down in her car before dropping me home on a bitterly cold day after I'd wet myself because I forgot to go during lunchtime. Bed wetter, car wetter and now, please God no, not shop wetter.

16:05

I just make it. I'm lucky. It's almost as if my fat lump of a body has decided that it has been through too much already today. The only thing that's worrying me now is that the 'ahhhhhhhhh' that I involuntarily blurted out when I ripped off the pink poncho has been heard in the shop.

16:07

I have no other option. I have to carry the weighted vest out with me instead of wearing it and dump the pink poncho. When I eventually clean myself up, I walk out into the shop with a soaked T-shirt, carrying the weighted vest.

16:09

The shop assistant points to the weighted vest and asks me, in complete seriousness, 'Did you get that here?'

16:10

I am now walking down Baggot Street in Dublin, carrying the weighted vest, wearing jeans and a drenched T-shirt while trying to hold up an umbrella.

17:10

I eventually reach my car in the Park. By the time I get into the driver's seat, every bone in my body hurts. Then I can feel an overwhelming surge of sickness. I open the car door and puke onto the grass verge. The clay is coming out of me like lava from a volcano. Now all I can taste is the clay. Every time I think I'm finished getting sick, I can taste the clay again and more comes up. I actually think I might be dying. I'm also checking to see if I did my step count. I'm presuming that if you're checking your step count you are probably not dying. This is a bizarre comfort to me.

17:25

My wife has picked up the kids and has rung me to tell me there is no bread or milk in the house. I look at myself in the car's vanity mirror. I look like I've just come back from a World War I trench and the thought of having to go to the shop fills me with dread. I start thinking, if I did come back from war, instead of throwing her arms around me, the first thing my wife would probably say to me is 'There's no milk or bread in the house – go to the shop.'

17:55

I'm standing at the self-service checkout in the supermarket. I don't have a bag. The machine tells me to 'Place bag on counter'. There is no button to tell it, 'I don't have a bag'. I try to place the milk, bread, bananas, apples and toilet roll (Lorna had texted me extra items to get) onto the area. The screen tells me again, 'Place bag on counter'. Eventually a shop assistant comes over and swipes her magic-barcode lanyard like a lightsabre at the screen. The self-service till shrieks and allows me to 'place item on checkout counter' without having a bag.

17:55:16

The screen tells me again: 'Place item on checkout counter'. I'm now trying to make eye contact with the shop assistant again. I pick up the bananas and scan them again. It then tells me to 'place item on checkout counter' once more.

17:55:45

The shop assistant tames the snarky tiger of a screen again and once more, I am free to scan my items.

17:55:57

The screen will not relinquish the fight: 'Place item on checkout counter'.

17:56:02

I want to crawl into a hole. I feel like walking away. Everybody is looking at me. Now I'm the guy holding up the queue. I pick up the items and walk to a till that has a human behind it.

17:58:02

'Do you need a bag?' says the friendly checkout assistant.

I want to reply, 'I actually need somebody to sort my entire fucking life out. To tell me how to parent. To tell me why I eat tubs of ice-cream mindlessly at night while gorging on box sets that I forget instantly. To tell me why I'm only happy when I'm plastered drunk. I need someone to explain why I feel like taking up smoking again every time I hear my name being mentioned, good or bad. I need to understand why I check my phone every 30 seconds. I need to understand why I constantly tell myself I'm not anxious or watch countless videos of Swedish men waxing work trousers. Why I need to keep buying various pieces of moulded plastic on Amazon that promise me I'll live longer. Why I need to swallow dirt – actual dirt – to help me lose weight. I probably need to live in Connemara with the family and bake soda bread and chop wood. Do I need a bag?'

Taking a deep breath in, I reply, 'No thanks.'

18:00

As I fumble the shopping onto the passenger seat of the car, I hear the church bells ringing in the local church. I mumble to myself, 'What a total waste of time you are.'

18:16

I eventually get home.

PART THREE

The Devil You Know

My plan was just beginning, but it was already failing – and failing miserably. My Weight, Fitness and Mind were in worse shape than ever. I needed to reckon with the biggest obstacle in my path: myself.

For two years I had walked the same way to the train station so, one time, as I was leaving the office, I decided to go a different way. I walked down Dublin's Kildare Street flush with positivity. I was happy with my plan and I seemed to be almost calm. I began thinking, 'I bet it's because I've written my plan down, or maybe it's just the thought of going to Mass again. Maybe it's given me some divine apparition of peace.' Either way, I felt good. Leinster House and the National Museum are both on Kildare Street and as I was passing the museum, I saw a familiar face. I caught his eye and he went, 'Ah, Bernard.' He reached out his hand and I started to shake it. My mind started racing trying to figure out what my friend's name was.

'What are you doing here?' he said. I still couldn't remember his name.

'Oh, I have an office around the corner.' He was still shaking my hand. So, I said the first thing that came into my mind: 'They have lovely muffins in the museum café.'

He paused and looked at me like a man would at another man who's just said, 'They have lovely muffins in the museum café.' I could see that I had put him in an awkward position, so I tried to fix it. 'You're looking fantastic.' Oh, Jesus, what did I say that for?

'You're looking well yourself,' he replied.

Then I began to get really f**king angry with my brain. I started to shout at it: 'TELL ME WHO THIS PERSON IS?' I kept looking at his face. It was, in the nicest way, the most normal face on the planet. Everything was in proportion. The one benefit of an Irish face is that there is always a bit of craziness going on. I worked in a hotel once with three Russian women. One of them said to me, 'Irish are beautiful but mostly on the inside.' But this guy's face had no botched planning permissions. Normally you'd get an oversized nose or one ear bigger than the other, but this face was normal. He had brownish-grey receding hair and I was trying to compute as quickly as possible what he would look like with a full head of hair to see if I could jog my memory.

He was now staring at me. I was about to give in and just ask him to tell me who he was and then he said, 'Jesus, I'd say the last time I was here [the museum] we would have been in school.' That was it – school! I must have gone to school with him. But, on second thoughts, there were only ten in my primary school class, so it must have been secondary school. The feeling of relief spread across my brain, like a warm electric blanket on your big toe on a cold wet night. I remembered him. I just couldn't remember his name. 'God, how are you?' I said.

Now, I rarely ask other people this question, because I am obsessed with myself. For years, I tried to deny it, until somebody drunkenly said to me at a wedding: 'Do you want to ask me how I am?' I love to talk. I talk for a living. It's just that I love talking about myself. My wife, when quizzed about me, says, 'Everybody's favourite subject is themselves, but Bernard brings it to a whole new level.' But today I was in a good mood, so I asked him how he was, expecting a quick answer and then I would be on my way.

What I got was basically the guy's life story. He told me about working abroad. Getting married. Losing his job. Getting another job and finally, and very openly, he told me about the struggle he went through when he found out his wife was with another man. He very casually added, 'I still love her'.

'Jesus, that's terrible,' I said as I kept nodding my head. I had missed my train by this stage and knew I was probably late for the next one, too. I tried to get a quick glance at my watch without him noticing. He saw me and said, 'Oh, here, I don't want to keep you waiting.'

'No, no, no, not at all.' I was just about to tell him that it was great catching up and we must keep in contact, when he blurted out, 'Oh, here's my mother'. His mother approached carrying a golf bag, which was roughly the same size as her. She placed it on the path. She was the smallest person I have ever seen in my life. I couldn't help thinking, how did she give birth to my long-lost friend, whose name I've forgotten?

'Would you believe,' she started, 'I carried that from the bus on O'Connell Street all the way here and he [pointing at her son] doesn't even play golf.' And then, the most spine-tinglingly excruciating thirty seconds of my life began. My newfound friend said nothing! What was I supposed to do? I didn't know his name or his mother's. She looked at me, expecting me to say something. He just happily stared at me with a stupid grin on his face. I thought about doing a little hop and skip to get me off the ground while saying something bland like 'Nice meeting you, have to go', but they had actually corralled me in, she with her tiny frame, him with his silent head, and the golf bag blocking the exit.

Eventually she said, 'Are you going to introduce me to your friend?' Every living cell of my body stood to attention, like a satellite dish waiting to receive information. She was going to reveal his name. His name, that when I heard it, I was going to repeat it to him again and again to make it look like I hadn't forgotten it. 'Well, are you, ya big lump?'

What, I thought, she didn't say his name? 'You big lump'? One hundred per cent worse now. Eventually, he spoke. 'Oh, this is Bernard, Mum.'

'And how do you know each other?' she said.

Silence. He stood there, in fairness to his mother, like a big lump. I eventually had to say, 'We went to school together', then instantly he replied, 'No we didn't.'

Now, I was totally thrown. 'How do you know me then?'

He looked at me and said, 'From the telly.'

His mother then added, 'Gregory [no use to me now], do you want this thing' – she pointed to the golf bag – 'or not?'

I started to walk away, saying, 'Nice to meet you, Gregory, I hope everything works out for you.'

His mother suddenly exploded, like a colonial cannon: 'What have you been telling this fella? Just because he knows you from the telly doesn't mean you can go and make a skit out of his life.'

At this stage, all I could think of was, how do I get out of this situation? 'Look,' I said, 'this has been a misunderstanding. I will not be making a "skit" out of anything. I have to go.'

Then, out of the blue, she said, 'You're very heavy. You looked a lot lighter on the telly.'

I was shocked. My brain actually started firing out the f-bomb, but my new friend Gregory said, 'Mum, that's rude.'

'No, it isn't. I'm just saying he looked a lot smaller on the telly.'

Eventually, I felt I had permission to walk away. I could hear him shout in the distance: 'Bernard, Bernard, Bernard.'

I turned and he ran up to me. 'Could we get a selfie?'

When I got home, I told my wife the story. 'I don't believe you,' she said.

'What?' I was flabbergasted. 'Why would I lie about something like that? Why would I lie about thinking I knew someone then being accosted by his mother carrying a golf bag? Why would I do that?'

Then she rolled out her punchline. 'You lie for a living, Bernard, and you lie all the time.'

I constantly have this argument with Lorna. I don't lie all the time. I bend the truth at times to protect people or to get a laugh.

She continued, 'You can do all the fad diets in the world, but you are just going to lie to yourself about the results as well.'

I shot back with my current plan, to which she replied, 'So, you are going to eat clay and walk to Mass with a weighted vest on? That's your plan? You are actually lying to yourself now, Bernard.'

I wasn't having this. I was trying to be a better person, to improve myself for everybody's sake and now I was being accused of being nothing more than a professional liar. I wheeled out Lorna's weapon of choice when it comes to arguments: 'Be specific. Give me SPECIFIC times when I lied?'

I shouldn't have. She began describing what she eventually coined 'six of the best':

LIE NUMBER 1

'You lied about your age to the therapist the time we got a couples' massage.'

When you have kids, life, and most definitely weekends, change. You can no longer just decide to pop off aimlessly for a couple of days. My wife isn't an 'aimless' type anyway. She has always planned out any kind of adventure. She once told me that she would love to just get in the car and go – with no plan – but when I did this one day with her, she absolutely freaked and started telling me to go back to the house immediately. Eventually, after six hours of packing and extensive googling, she had decided exactly where our 'get in the car and go anywhere' weekend was going to be.

I'm not that that type. I'll happily go anywhere with anyone. My mother jokes that she's amazed I didn't go missing as a child, as I would have wandered anywhere. My happy-go-lucky attitude is strongly punctuated by having no sense of direction whatsoever. Without my phone or satnav, I would honestly be dead. I once got stuck in an outdoor car park, to the anger and amusement of my wife. Unless I'm with other people, I have to turn on maps on my phone in the car for even the simplest journey. I've spent way too many hours driving around suburbia – once, I ended up driving on a road with grass in the middle of it because I was convinced 'I know where I am now'. Technology is quite literally my best friend. I once drove to Galway instead of Belfast and Belfast instead of Galway in one week. I constantly miss major turn-offs on motorways, and I have got trains and buses home because I've forgotten where I parked my car. It once took me two hours to drive fifteen miles because I kept getting off at the wrong exit on a roundabout. One of my wife's many nicknames for me is 'Circles' – because I keep walking or driving in circles.

But our main bone of contention is where we park. I like to find a spot with loads of room that I can pull into and out of handily. However, she basically wants to park in the shop. 'Why do you always have to park so far away?' she complains. 'We're miles from the shops.' This particularly does my head in as she will often bemoan the fact that there are days she 'can't even get out for a walk' when she's at home.

So, one weekend, when my wife wanted to nip into a supermarket in an area of Dublin I wasn't familiar with, I turned on my satnav in the car park. She thought this was hilarious. I found a spot right outside the quintessentially 1980s-style shopping centre. I stayed in the car and waited for her return. Half an hour later, she remerged, stocked with 'essentials' for her carefully planned, carefree, go-anywhere weekend. Even though I've no sense of direction, I'm a stickler for the rules, especially traffic signs. Lorna, on the other hand, always ignores the carefully planned exits and entrances in car parks. In this unfamiliar car park, I went in a clockwise direction twice in search of the exit, to find out that I kept ending up in the same place.

Then it started. 'You lost, Circles?' The only option I felt I had was to drive through a little walkway I'd spotted, or else, I'd have to drive through the main barrier that was only for incoming cars. As I was driving towards it, Lorna screamed, 'BERNARD, THAT'S THE EXIT OVER THERE.' It was too late. The walkway was too narrow, and the car got stuck so I ended up jammed into the shopping centre's pedestrian entrance.

For a few seconds, it looked like the car was one of those promotional ones that they often display in shopping centres, and we were simply the idiots who'd got into it. I could see the security guard walking in my direction. Lorna's expression was a mix of uncontrollable laughter and disappointment (a look I'm quite used to seeing). I told the security guard that the clockwise layout of the car park didn't work and there was no exit in plain view. He told me that it had worked for 30 years and that I was the first person who'd ever tried to drive into the tiny gap that was the pedestrian entrance.

Eventually, every man in his 60s congregated around my car and had an opinion on how to get me out. It's possibly the most difficult thing in the world to try and reverse with loads of people 'helping you', or interjecting with phrases like 'How did he manage that?' Lorna had, by this stage, managed to climb out of the car. I could see her laughing in the background. Eventually I got the car out, having scratched all four doors.

From that day on, we decided to implement the Driver Rule: neither of us will critique the other's driving if we're in the passenger seat. However, we are now a far cry from being able to take off any weekend, aimlessly or not.

When you have your first child, you protect it, like a Murano glass figurine. Your second comes along, and you now have two Waterford Crystal wine glasses. Your third arrives and you have three pint glasses. It also becomes next-or-near impossible to ask people to look after three kids under six. However, Nanna and Grandad are very obliging and so, nearly three-and-a-half years after our last weekend, myself and Lorna were on the road again for a two-night spa retreat that we had copious amounts of vouchers for.

Over the last few years, we have entered what I like to call 'The Voucher Zone'. Every birthday I give Lorna a voucher for a spa I know she likes, and she says, 'How am I supposed to go, Bernard?' Then I mention to my family that I've got her the aforementioned voucher. Then my family members will get me a voucher for the same place for my birthday, so now we've ended up having six vouchers for the same spa hotel collected over a three-year period. Go to any weekend retreat and you'll find it full of sleep-deprived parents. You'll also hear, fluttering over the scented breeze, the words 'We had vouchers we had to use up.'

So, there we were, heading away together ON OUR OWN. As always, I entered the address into the satnav and within 40 minutes we were lost. Ireland is still treated with contempt by the internet and our new motorways don't always pop up on maps. So, for the best part of half an hour I drove through a virtual field. Eventually we found the hotel. First impressions – it was very posh. One of these places that you know the staff will look at you and think 'they are lost'.

Before I got out of the car, we were met at the door by somebody who tried to steal my car! Oh no, wait, by a valet. Then another man came and took our luggage – I was to find out later that they are called bell boys. The interior of the hotel was decorated in the style of *Grand Design's* Kevin McCloud's home: all modern furniture and abstract art. The first thing I thought was something I'd normally say to the kids if we were in a nice shop: 'Don't touch anything.' I also took a mental note not to get drunk or walk anywhere for fear of adding what looked like several thousands of euro to our bill.

We went to check in but neither of us could find the check-in desk. This seems to be a new thing in the hotel trade, especially when the establishment wants to create an 'experience'. Usually, I stay in hotels where the check-in desk is very much a 'check-in desk'. You say your name, they give you a white or black plastic card and, if you are like me, you wander around aimlessly for fifteen minutes before you find your room. For some reason, I always get rooms with numbers like 16A or 134C. It's almost as if they see me coming and think, 'This fella looks like he has no sense of direction – let's give him the room on the first floor that is actually on the second.' However, posh hotels don't go in for that redundant behaviour. Their check-in desk is always positioned lengthways facing you, so that you don't know what side you should wait on. There's normally an Italian-style couch that only a yoga instructor would be able to sit on comfortably and there are rugs: lots and lots of rugs.

Lorna and I were eventually asked to sit down to get checked in. This procedure always makes me feel as if I'm going for mortgage approval or for a counselling session. A very pretty woman ushered us to a Bauhaus-style bench, and she started to ask us questions like 'Did you have a nice journey here?'

Now, I know they probably have to ask this, but I tried to answer it as brilliantly as I could because I immediately felt intimidated by her good looks and perfect BMI. 'Eh, yeah … yes, thank you. We travelled by the motorway … we came from Dublin. Traffic was light and …' My wife interrupted with, 'Yes, thank you.'

The receptionist continued: 'My name is Monica and I'll be checking you in this evening and answering any questions you have.' She started to tell us all about the spa and asked us if we had any treatments booked in. Lorna answered yes and then Monica looked at me and said, 'And you, sir, have you booked any treatments?' Now, if I was completely honest with Monica I would have told her that I planned on getting drunk and sleeping in the next day, but because I felt like a fifteen-year-old trying to impress a good-looking temp teacher I said, 'No, actually I wanted to get an opinion on that.'

Again, my wife interrupted: 'We have booked a couple's mud chamber.' I laughed out loud only to instantly catch Lorna's placid facial expression, indicating that this wasn't a joke.

Monica finished typing on the keyboard and looked up 'Oh, that will be nice for the two of you. Your room will be ready very shortly – would you like to relax in our bar area?' The one thing that bugs the absolute shit out of me is this: since when can you not go to the room before 2 or 3 pm, but have to be out by twelve noon the following day, or else the Gestapo come and hunt you out by banging a vacuum cleaner against the door? I know why you can't check-in if they don't have the rooms, but I hate the feeling of thinking I am going to be lying in a nice hotel bed but instead having to walk sheepishly up to reception every twenty minutes to ask if the room is ready.

My wife knows this bugs me, so she quickly intercepted Monica's kind words: 'Yes, we will wait in the bar.'

Into the bar we trotted, and I could quickly see the difference between this and your normal Irish bar. Almost every Irish bar in the world has bookshelves, but they are only for decoration. It's very rarely you see a barman dealing with a customer asking, 'Do you have anything by Salman Rushdie?' However, this was different. There were real books on the shelves and people were reading them. 'You know what this means,' my brain said: 'You don't get drunk here.' I drink too quickly. I always have. I get so excited at the prospect of drinking alcohol that I normally get drunk within the hour and fall asleep quickly. It's not necessarily a bad thing. I go home earlier but don't remember anything of the night. I'm like a kid at a birthday party who eats all the sugar at his disposal as quickly as possible then completely crashes in a ball of tears and his mother has to bring him home. Just replace his mother with a taxi and that's me.

I can't drink any more. The hangovers are just too much. Now, I wake up the morning after and try not to move. If you move even your small toe, the hangover will begin. I get thirsty but just can't face getting out of the bed, so, I do what generations before me have done: I try to manoeuvre my tongue around in my mouth to locate as much moisture as it possibly can. Everyone does this, even Bono. I'm sure Obama has been on a night out and can't be arsed to get up and get a glass of water. Once, after a night out, I fell back asleep and dreamed that I'd got out of bed and got a glass of water. (That's what I dream about now – not playing Wembley Arena or winning an Oscar – I dream about getting fluids.)

However, true to form, while waiting in the bar, I got a bit tipsy. I couldn't help myself. Lorna had booked our spa treatment for later that day and said, 'You can't be drunk for it. It could be dangerous.' I told her to relax, then I'm pretty sure I lost about an hour because all I can remember is that we eventually checked into our room and I flopped onto the bed. 'Come on, we are going to be late. I'll meet you down there,' Lorna said. I didn't want to miss the treatment, but I knew I was drunk. Not tipsy, but drunk. Really drunk. Also, I didn't know what to wear. I never know what to wear in these places. If you go with just the bathrobe they provide, you look fine in the spa but then if you have my sense of direction, you could end up a semi-naked man trying to find room 13F on the 16th hole of a golf course. As I'm also big-boned, or fat, if you prefer, I'm conscious of my weighty frame. So, I eventually decided to wear a swimsuit, under a tracksuit, under the robe and I followed Lorna to the spa.

I can never settle in spa resorts. I always look at others and think they know what they are doing, while I always end up climbing into some water bath and getting stuck until somebody tells me it's for your feet only. Once I was told that the ice I'd been given wasn't for my rum and Coke, but to rub over my skin after the sauna. What's more, I was told, I wasn't allowed alcoholic drinks in the steam room. No matter how *au fait* Irish people are with fancy hotel spas, it still takes a foreigner to use something properly for us to go, 'Ah, that's how you use it'. It's not that we are uncultured – it's just not us. If you flip it, it's like watching a French or American tourist put blackcurrant into Guinness.

I had learned my lesson from previous encounters with the world of steam and verrucas and this time, I wisely brought a bottle of water and my flip-flops with me from the room. I couldn't see Lorna, so I headed into the sauna. I know that all you have to do there is sit, so I felt safe that I couldn't be a health spa philistine there. So safe, in fact, that I fell asleep.

'Get up, get up, get up, BERNARD.' I opened my eyes to find my wife poking me in the shoulder. 'I told you not to get to get drunk, you prick.'

I stood up and whacked my head off the sauna ceiling. 'I'm not drunk, I'm resting.'

'Come on, our treatment is beginning.' Normally, Lorna would never wait for me anywhere or for anything but possibly because the treatments had been booked with vouchers for both of us it skewed her decision to involve me. As we were getting the couple's mud-chamber treatment, we headed to that part of the spa and were shown into a small room. The therapist was a friendly woman, who asked us to fill out two simple questionnaires. 'Do you have any heart issues?' she enquired.

'It has been broken several times by several beautiful women,' I said, thinking it was the funniest thing I'd ever said in my life. However, she didn't quite understand me and asked, 'It's broken?'

'No,' I replied, 'I just meant that … no, I have no heart issues.'

'Is this an anniversary?' the woman asked.

Lorna smiled and said, 'No, but it was my birthday last week.'

The woman then looked at me. 'Aren't you lucky? You have such a beautiful young wife.'

Now, the best answer here, no matter what, is to say, 'YES'. There actually is no other answer to this question. But as I have a tendency to do, I danced wildly between the grey lines and replied, 'There are actually only three years between us.' That is technically a lie. There are five years between us, but it's part of a silly game I play with Lorna, jibing over our age gap. She hates it, but even so, I don't see it as a lie.

We were then given pots of mud to rub into our skin. I looked at the mud and asked the therapist, 'What does this do?' She told me quietly, in the tone of a librarian in a 1980s high school film, 'The mud is rich in natural elements and used to exfoliate and nourish the skin.' She left us to splatter ourselves in it. Once we'd done this, she returned and brought us into a steam room where we sat for half an hour. Then she came back and offered us moist towels and we cleaned ourselves off. I did notice I was extremely relaxed, and my skin did feel nice, but still, all I could think of was, how on earth did humans find out that this was good for you? It's like the age-old question of who was the first person to drink cow's milk and, more importantly, why?

As I was walking back after the treatment, I did notice that I was the biggest person in the spa. Quite literally, I was the largest person in the hotel. It was not the mud or steam that sobered me up but my size.

When I got back to the room, Lorna was waiting. 'It does my head in when you lie about my age. Lie about yours, that's fine, but not mine,' she said.

'I'm only kidding,' I said.

'Well, don't,' she snapped.

'I'm surprised you're touchy about it,' I laughed.

Instantly she shot back, 'Well, I'm surprised you found your own way back to the room.'

LIE NUMBER 2
'You lied about going hiking to that sales assistant.'

Among the shoes that lie dormant in my car boot are a pair of €280 hiking boots. I've always had visions of myself as a mountain climber. Just me and a windswept mountain and a flask of tea. I envision myself on the top looking down over a landscape newly conquered, because of my natural ability to reach soaring heights. In reality, I like the odd walk. I walk in the park close to my home, which is flat. On a good day, I do about two miles. Hiking is not the only hobby I daydream about doing though. (I know, it's odd to 'daydream' about doing hobbies that you could actually do.) My other daydream hobbies are car racing, flying a plane and doing sculpture. The problem with car racing, flying a plane and doing sculpture is that each requires me to either do some training or to buy a plane, race car or some marble. With hiking, you can essentially just, well … go for a hike.

If that is to happen to me, I will be well equipped. I have loads of outdoor clothes in my wardrobe. In fact, most days, when I leave the house, I'm wearing the kind of Gore-Tex outfits that Sherpa Tensing could have only dreamed of when he and Edmund Hillary stepped onto the summit of Everest for the first time. I have rain jackets that not alone repel water but are also 'breathable'. I have socks that are made from lambswool and are engineered to not chafe my delicate feet and I own several pairs of Woodman outdoor trousers with pouches in them for Bowie knives. However, they have never been put to the test except in a very mild shower of rain in my local park.

I've a problem with buying outdoor survival clothes, in the same way that some women have a problem with only buying leisure wear, because they obsess over yoga. I'll be treading a perfectly engineered footpath with a North Face jacket and Thinsulate-lined boots, when I'll think, I need some breathable mosquito-proof pants. Along with my beige splurge, I've started to buy waxed clothes. There is something about applying the wax that makes me think I'm fighting the wild. I have, however, destroyed two irons in doing so. Now my wife hides the iron: 'You can pretend to be Bear Grylls with your own iron, Bernard, the kids' clothes are covered in wax.' One of the more embarrassing moments of recent times was when my wife burst into the bedroom to see me naked on the bed watching the laptop. When she heard a deep male voice speaking in Swedish she said, 'Are you watching Swedish men put wax on their trousers again?' I was.

I am amazing, though, at putting picnics together. I always cut the sandwiches in quarters and bring diluted orange in a flask instead of tea. The kids think it's amazing. If I'm ever stuck in a snow shower in the tundra, I know I won't starve. I'll have a flask of orange and a packet of ham sandwiches laid out on a traditional herringbone-tweed blanket instead of raw seal livers on nettles.

A walking lifeline was thrown to me when Ronan, a friend

of mine from college, told me that I could join him on a mountain walk some weekend.

'Aren't you a part of a club?' I asked him.

'Yeah, but. . . ' he hesitated a bit, 'you'd want to be going for a while … it can be tough.'

I started laughing. 'You're joking – I can walk for a long time.'

He stopped me there. 'It's not how far you can walk. Hiking is different. The first few times I went out, I was in bits. They keep a fast pace and you're going up all the time. I'll bring you on a moderate hike and then see.' We ventured onto a different topic but then he said: 'I have a walking stick you can borrow.'

I erupted. 'A stick? I'm not ninety years of age. I don't need a stick to go for a walk.'

He quickly interrupted me, 'That's the difference between a hike and a walk, you'll need a stick for a hike.'

But in my head, I had already made the decision. 'I'm not going anywhere with a walking stick.'

My conversation with Ronan, however, was a perfect start to another feast of spending. This time my brain had zeroed in on hiking boots. I googled them relentlessly and eventually found a specialised shop in a shopping centre on the south side of Dublin. When I was growing up, there was the Scout shop in Dublin and that was it. It mostly sold thick bin liners that you could sleep in, called Bivvy Bags, gas stoves and tent pegs. There were also army surplus stores. They didn't sell much army equipment, rather outdated uniforms; they mostly sold the grunge look to Nirvana fans. For four years in secondary school most of us looked like a small division of the West German army who'd grown their hair long.

However, there must be a lot of people like me around today because you can get any outdoor equipment imaginable in your average shopping centre. Any hobby you have, you can buy an accessory for it. I remember when I was seven years of age, myself and my friend used to play tennis on the road outside our house. I used a small coal shovel as my racket. Thank God I never qualified for Wimbledon, as I would have brought the Irish nation to shame if I showed up on Centre Court with my small black shovel. My mother would have killed me as well, as she would constantly shout, 'Bernard, put back that shovel.' Now, hobbies for kids are organised. My kids think it's insane that we played on the road. Now I freak out if Olivia, who is six, walks on the footpath without holding my hand. My mother once remarked that when I was six, a group of us cycled to a village five miles away to a swimming pool. The gem is that none of us could swim.

One Saturday morning we corralled the kids into the car, strapped them in and headed for a shopping centre in search of hiking boots. Prior to having kids, I used to look at families in shopping centres and think to myself, I will never bring my kids shopping and force them to trawl after us in artificially lit white-walled colosseums. I envisioned myself bringing the kids to parks and flying kites. Little did I know that any outdoor activity with children has the potential to end in tears, hospital visits and screams – lots of screams. In my mind, I would be that slim, attractive man frolicking through the park, laughing with my toddlers, showing them how to fly a kite and relishing teaching them in the outdoors every weekend. In reality, I'm an overweight man-child in a shopping centre, who constantly has to roar at the kids that 'WE ARE NOT GOING BACK TO THE NUTELLA STAND' while also saying, over and over again, 'Do any of ye need to go to the toilet? If you do, GO NOW.' I am that man who has a screaming child with him at the toy-shop entrance.

The thing is, I've swapped my hobbies for shopping centres. Shopping centres are essentially churches of handiness. They are so handy with kids: they can't run away, there are toilets, shops and copious amounts of sugar. However, I am also one of those parents who is guilt-ridden about them eating candy floss for lunch. So, to all those parents I sniffed at and thought were just lazy for blocking up the queues to Pizza Hut on Saturdays, I apologise.

However, the day we went to get my hiking boots, one of the most embarrassing parenting moments of my parenting life occurred.

We decided that we would do our 'big shop' in the supermarket and afterwards, I could go on my own to the outdoor shop, while Lorna looked after the kids. After the two-hour-long struggle of dragging the kids around food aisles, Lorna brought Olivia and Tadhg (this was before Seán's arrival) to a play zone. I ventured forth into the wild … well, the outdoor and adventure shop. This shop had a climbing wall in it. I remember once being on a climbing wall in Dublin's Trinity College. They were taking publicity photos for a TV campaign and I got my testicles caught in the climbing harness. The pain was bad, but the thought of having to get out of the harness and prolong the shoot meant that I stayed suspended in the thing, literally by my testicles, for an hour. It's a statement that a lot of these shops now make: 'LOOK AT US. WE HAVE A CLIMBING WALL. THIS IS A SERIOUS OUTDOOR SHOP.' All the staff looked like they had just come back from a rock wall and camping expedition that Friday. Now they were busy looking after middle-aged men pretending they needed waterproof Gore-Tex hiking boots.

I looked around and was genuinely gobsmacked and impressed by the place. There were pictures everywhere of explorers on white peaks wearing snow goggles and pointing off into the distance. They also had an entire wall laden with walking sticks, which I now learned were called 'poles'. I thought back to my conversation with Ronan. If I wanted to look serious, I probably needed a pole.

There was a section just for 'trail running'. Up until that very second, I hadn't known that trail running was a thing. Surely if you are running quickly in a forest, going up or down a mountain trail, you have murdered someone? Apparently not. This is a hobby: running in places where it is impossible to run. I couldn't get my head around it. It would be like saying, 'I like to recite the works of Shakespeare in fast-food restaurants when the pubs close.' Doable, but very difficult, and would probably end in you getting a bone broken.

It wasn't long before I was approached by a sales assistant. He was young, possibly in his early twenties, and had a perfectly shaped head. He had chalk dust on his hands as he had casually propelled himself off the climbing wall to come to my assistance. He looked like he had the option of either working here or as one of those lads who have their tops off in Abercrombie & Fitch. He puffed out his chest and blurted 'Help?'

This is where my pity for the struggle of the Millennial ends: 'Help?' is not a sentence, but it was more the way it was said that bothered me. Now before I start, I want to make one thing very clear. This is not me saying he was aggressive or unhelpful – it is simply that he spoke in McGregorish. This is a patois that young adults use. Conor McGregor is possibly the most famous Irishman of this century. He has won several UFC world championships in mixed martial arts. He comes from a working-class background and worked unbelievably hard to achieve domination in his sport. His personality is brash, arrogant, at times aggressive: it matches a sport that is dangerous, with high stakes, but it's HIS personality. However, his persona has somehow made its way into the heads of nearly every young man who knows what a bench press is.

The way this young man said, 'Help?' was annoying but something I could understand. Young people especially need role models. Nowadays, you have masses of highly educated kids with a knowledge of nutrition, Mindfulness and ambition to burn who keep hitting glass ceilings. They try to get jobs and end up as 'interns'. They have been squeezed out of the housing market, so they have been brainwashed into having 'experiences' instead. Basically, this is shorthand for, 'Not able to get a mortgage? Spend your money on experiences instead!' When they come back to Dublin from finding themselves in Thailand or wrecking Australia, they have to go into a low-paid job so they can afford to buy lunch twice a week and then they end up moving in with their parents again and having to jump off a climbing wall to assist a fat red-haired man who will never use the crap he's going to buy. Why would he be bothered using a full sentence, when 'Help?' is all he's really being paid for? The rest of the sentence can wait.

But for some reason, for the first time in my life, when that shop assistant said 'Help?' I felt like screaming: 'YOU'RE NOT CONOR MCGREGOR. YOU'RE FROM MIDDLE-CLASS DUBLIN. YOUR MUM IS PROBABLY GOING TO PICK YOU UP LATER.' I was completely enraged by the way he said it. I came within seconds of saying, 'Young man, I don't like your tone.' I was trying to configure my emotions in my head and came to a shuddering realisation:

I felt threatened by a younger man. Forget the clothes, the weight, the bad knees, the feeling that most music in pubs 'is too loud' – this moment made me feel old. I looked at him. Brash, confident, symmetrical and thin, and I thought, 'This is what I really want,' not a hiking shoe. I want to be in my twenties. I want his hair because it isn't receding. I want his upper chest which isn't floppy and his stomach, which he doesn't have to suck in every time he meets someone new. If I were a vampire, I'd suck his blood, pay with my credit card and leave. For all this time I had convinced myself that I was happy in the newly conquered beige paradise of my 40s, but I wasn't. I had a genuine religious experience in an outdoor shop beside a rack selling gas canisters. I wanted my youth back.

But the anger ignition button had been pressed in my brain and I stared him down and snapped, 'I'm looking for the rest of that sentence.' He gave me a blank look. I barked again, 'Do you know where you put the rest of the sentence? Like, "Do you want any … help?"'

He looked blankly at me again. 'Sorry, what?'

'You said, "Help". I'm presuming you could have said, "Would you like some help?"'

He said, 'I was calling for help from another staff member. I need someone to keep an eye on the climbing wall.' It was then I saw he was wearing one of those earphones and had a little cable clipped onto his shirt. Another moment in my life where my temper has made a complete idiot of me. 'Oh, yeah,' I said and went straight into denial mode. I started talking to him as if it had never happened. 'I'm looking for a new trekking boot.' I said 'new' because there was still no way I was going to let him know I was a newbie.

'Oh, so what were you wearing before?'

Oh, shite, that's a very good question. 'What was I wearing before?' I randomly scanned the boots on display and said the first brand I saw: 'Hi-Tec … I had a pair of them.'

'Which ones?' He was like an enthusiastic puppy. 'The Altitude Four or the Storm Series?'

Now, here's the problem I have with lying. I feel that, if you're going to lie, you should be allowed at least a fifteen-minute grace period before you're asked tricky questions. 'Eh … I think I had the Storm.'

'You *think*?' he said. 'Were they leather or Gore-Tex?'

Ah, for f**k's sake, how much does this guy know about hiking shoes? I gambled on leather.

'That would have been the Altitude; they are famous for being leather.'

Yeah, I'm sure they are, Rock Boy, I thought.

He continued, 'If you're looking for something to just walk in the park [which I kind of was] I'd look at a good waterproof walking shoe. These are more for serious hiking,' he said, pointing to the Altitudes.

It was the phrase 'serious hiking' that got me. He didn't know that I wasn't a 'serious hiker'. He just took one look at me and presumed I was some overweight idiot who thought that hiking would be their ticket to weight loss. He was a hundred per cent right. But then he really pissed me off: 'Come over here, buddy, I'll show you some stuff that will probably suit you better.'

I wasn't backing down. As far as this twenty-something was concerned, I was a mountain goat. I confidently announced, 'No, I'm looking for a serious hiking boot actually. I'm a member of a hiking club.'

'OK, no problem. What are you carrying?'

'What am I carrying?'

'Yeah, are you backpacking? You had the Altitude, so I presume you're looking for hi-tops with load resistance.'

So, he had me straight away. I just had to remember enough of what he'd said or steer him in another direction. 'I'm looking for that but with possible … options.'

'Options?'

'Yeah, like, eh …'

'Do you mean you're looking for a lightweight hi-top with deep lugs?'

At this stage, if I was in a fighter jet, I would have pressed the ejector-seat button. I hadn't a clue what 'lugs' were, and he knew it.

'Yeah.'

'I always say you are better off with the deep lugs.'

'I think so, too.'

'Your load capacity will be compromised though.'

'Yeah, but I'll deal with that compromise,' I said confidently.

He got a little step ladder and pulled down a black and red pair of boots that looked like they came from the costume department of a *Star Wars* film. 'These are the latest in breathable Gore-Tex and have a new vibrate composite sole.' As he was showing them to me, all I could think of was the step ladder. No matter how advanced we are as humans, at some point in our quest for technological advancement, we need a step ladder, whether it's getting out of Apollo 11 to walk on the moon for the first time or to show someone who's completely out of his depth the 'latest in breathable Gore-Tex'. I kept staring at that step ladder because I knew I had gone too far down the bullshit road. I just kept looking at that bright blue step ladder hoping that these boots cost less than a small car. They looked expensive and stupid. That is the best way to describe them … stupid. They had bright red writing down the side of them and a hook and clip system instead of laces. They were completely and utterly stupid. Not 'odd' or 'outrageous' or 'extravagant'. They were just stupid.

'Because these are the newest model, they are quite pricey.'

'How much are they?' I braced myself. I was in a trap. A trap I had made for myself, walked into myself and had thrown away the key to myself. 'Eh … [my heart was beating faster] these are … [I started to pray for the first time in twenty years] … they are two hundred and eighty euros.'

My heart actually skipped a beat. I was not spending €280 on boots that I knew would end up in the boot of my car along with the rest of my failed life.

There was a sizeable pause. I didn't want to back down. He spoke again. 'They are a serious piece of kit.'

There was that word 'serious'. As I've got older, I've come to truly understand old sayings like 'A bird in the hand is worth two in the bush', or 'The grass is always greener on the other side.' It's only experience that lets you fully understand those wise old proverbs. I was about to become the epitome of the saying 'Pride comes before a fall'. I felt that I stepped out of my body and was looking at a complete stranger doing the talking for me. 'Yeah, I'll take them.'

'Eh, do you not want to try them on first? You should.'

I knew I should but because there was no way I was ever going to let anybody see me in those stupid boots, I didn't need to try them on. Especially because I was wearing my beige khakis and a green knitted jumper. I would look like I had been attacked by the future from the soles up.

'I take them in a nine.'

'You really should try them on first.' He was insistent.

'I don't have much time – a size nine should be fine,' I replied.

'Honestly, man, you should try them on first.'

I gave in. He returned with the size nines. I put both of them on and walked up and down the tiny piece of carpet they had for middle-aged men to model their new footwear and their failed potential. I caught myself in the mirror and again the first thought I had was 'stupid'.

The assistant looked at me and explained, 'It's really important that you break them in first. Like, do a mile or two on a flat surface for a week or two. If you go uphill or for a long backpack without breaking them in, they will destroy your feet. They also come with a waterproof sealant. I'll just go get it.' He headed off again to the back room.

'Break them in,' I thought. He's not selling me a colt. All I wanted to do was get out of them, but I couldn't figure out how.

'Are you buying those?' I looked up and my wife and two kids had entered the shop. Within seconds, Tadhg was grabbing the boots and playing with the hooks. Whatever he did, he loosened them enough so that I was able to take them off.

Olivia screamed, 'Daddy they look MAD.'

Lorna, who normally never comments about anything I buy, said, 'They're not for normal wear, right?'

I was quick to answer her, as I wanted this disastrous overpriced shopping experience to be over. 'No, they are for hiking.' Then, like cosmic planets aligning in a galaxy of embarrassments, at the exact time Rock Boy re-entered the room, she snarled, 'You don't go hiking.'

The young assistant looked at her and said, 'Can I help you with anything?' This was unbelievable. Only ten minutes before, I'd got 'Help?' Now, he'd laid on the full sentence for my wife.

'No thanks, I think my husband is buying these . . . is he?' She laughed. In fact, she actually guffawed.

He smiled back at her. 'Well, he tells me he is a serious hiker.'

This was the final straw. Now I was being ridiculed while my wife flirted with a twenty-year-old. I put the boots into their bag (not a shoebox because apparently that doesn't work anymore in the world of footwear) and asked him if I could fix up.

Meanwhile, Olivia had seen the climbing wall and had started climbing up it like a monkey, followed by Tadhg, who was shouting at her, 'Go all the way up, Olivia.'

'I can take for them here,' he said.

Of course, he could 'take for them here'. Again, what's wrong with a till? My wife would know how much I'd be paying for them then. The thing is, we don't interfere with each other's money: we never have. If Lorna was to tell me she wanted to sell the house and everything we own to buy a designer handbag, I'd probably fight it for a few minutes, but I wouldn't care. It's only when we had kids that I started to worry about having money. I'm a spender. I can't keep money in my pocket. It's almost like a mental condition: I just can't stop spending whatever I earn. I can go without things, but kids like food, education and healthcare, so €280 for a pair of boots that are designed to do only one activity was lavish. Not to mention the fact that my wife had just told the world I had never hiked – just in case anyone else in the shop wanted to judge me.

She was a bit taken aback. 'Two hundred and eighty euro? Bernard, that's an awful lot of money for something you … mightn't use.' She was most definitely using the word 'mightn't' as a cautious replacement for 'won't'.

'I'll use them,' I quickly replied. I just wanted an exit now at any cost.

Rock Boy wasn't finished. 'When are you going out with your club again … what's the name? I know a lot of the clubs.'

Lorna looked at me: 'You're in a club?'

This just couldn't get worse. 'Yeah, with Ronan.'

She wrinkled her nose. 'Your friend Ronan who goes on the hill walks?'

'Yeah, Ronan, he goes hiking.'

Rock Boy was loving this. Along with his ridiculously tight T-shirt he was also wearing a big non-wrinkly smile on his youthful face.

Then Lorna dug the knife in deeper. 'What's the name of the club?' My brain went into overdrive. I couldn't think of anything. I was punching my 'think, brain, think' button. I then put it into 'desperate' mode, looking in every dusty corner of my mind for an answer. 'The Peak Climbers.' I don't know why I said it. It sounded right, though.

Then Rock Boy said, 'Normally it's just the area name. I've never heard of "The Peak Climbers". That sounds more like a mountaineering-club name. Is that their nickname?'

I decided to say nothing. Why should I answer him? Everybody knew that I was lying. I just wanted to get out of that shop. Luckily, Lorna lit that fuse for me. 'Come on, kiddos, let's go.' I grabbed my bag and Tadhg, but we were missing something … Olivia. She was way up high on the climbing wall shouting down, 'Look at me'. None of us had noticed how far up she'd gone.

Lorna called up to her, 'Come down, Olivia, now.'

Olivia came half-way down, just far enough for me to catch her. 'Can I stay for five more minutes, please?'

Then Rock Boy piped up: 'Do you like the climbing wall, Olivia?'

With a big scream she roared, 'Yeah it's great!'

Then Lorna appeared from nowhere, 'Do you climb often yourself?' she asked him.

He flexed his stupid neck muscles. 'Yeah, a fair bit. I try to get out as much as I can but it's hard with work.'

Tadhg was now at this guy's knee. 'Can you put me on the wall?' What was going on? Firstly, my wife had basically asked another man, in front of me, 'Do you come here often?' Now my son was latching onto this other man. *I'm* the guy for putting Tadhg on walls, not this Gore-Texed Millennial.

'Come on, guys, let's go,' I shouted. Now I was a man in a shop, shouting. 'No, Dad, please, just five more minutes,' Olivia begged. Tadhg was now changing tack, as he wanted to go to the toilet.

Lorna turned to Rock Boy. 'Nice meeting you. Come on, Tadhg.' Of course, Rock Boy had to be over-helpful, suggesting that there was a toilet beside the food court, and Lorna and Tadhg headed off.

'OK, Olivia,' I said. 'Five more minutes on the climbing wall.' She clambered back up to the top. Five minutes later she wanted 'just five more minutes, Dad, pleasssssssssse'. Eventually, I had to call time on her fun.

'I'M NOT GOING. YOU SAID FIVE MORE MINUTES,' she yelled.

I went straight into operation Over-Sugared Toddler. 'Olivia, we are leaving now,' I said in a low voice.

'I'm not going. Tadhg will be ages in the toilet.'

'Olivia,' I repeated, looking up at her, 'I'm warning you now … we are leaving.'

'I'm not going,' she replied. 'You said five more minutes.'

'I've already given you ten minutes.'

'Well, I asked for five.'

'No, I mean, you got two five minutes together.'

'Well, I only asked for five and you didn't give it to me then,' she said, looking down at me from her lofty perch.

It was time to bring out the big guns. 'Olivia, you are not getting movie night tonight,' I said. Movie night is basically where they watch a movie on Saturday nights. It is also somewhat of an excuse for them to squeeze out 'another five minutes' before going to bed.

When this didn't bring results, I said, 'Fine, have it your way so, Olivia. I'm going. I'll see you later. You can make your own way home and you will miss movie night.'

I like to call this the 'Tantrum Ransom'. If you have kids, or have ever been to an area where kids congregate with their sleep-deprived parents, i.e. zoos, Disneyland, Dinosaur Land, Peppa Land or anything ending in 'land' or 'zone', you will have probably witnessed the Tantrum Ransom. It's where a parent pretends to abandon their child by walking in the opposite direction in the hope that the child will run after them looking for forgiveness. I had never got to use it before, so I decided to give it a lash. It felt like being in school and being able to use a fire extinguisher for the first time in my life without the fear of being hauled into the principal's office.

I started to walk away. I kept walking, waiting for her to scream, 'No, Daddy, I love you too much, please wait for me.' By this stage I had walked as far as the shop door. I took a sneaky look around. She was still playing on the climbing wall. I knew I just had to leave the shop, then she would know I was serious. I did. I left the shop. I waited for her to scream. Nothing. I thought, if I go back in now, she wins. She will eventually break.

I waited. I stuck my head around the corner. There she was, still on the climbing wall. My phone rang and it was Lorna. I wasn't explaining this whole scenario to her, so I didn't answer. I went back in. 'Olivia, come on, this is enough, now we're leaving.'

'You said I could make my own way home,' she said.

Here's the thing: sometimes the Tantrum Ransom back-fires. Sometimes, the kid finds him- or herself in the exact position they want to be in. I had been out-manoeuvred by a six-year-old. I could have just carried her out screaming but I had had enough of the day. I had had enough of talking and looking at waterproof or water-resistant clothes. I had had enough of looking at a twenty-year-old trying to point me in the direction of something that would 'suit me better' as if he was trying to put me in a nursing home. I had had enough of my wife flirting with him. I just had enough.

So, I went nuclear on it. 'Olivia, if you leave now, I'll get you an ice-cream.'

She had climbed down the wall to the ground now. She stopped, folded her arms and said, 'I want the fluffy stuff from the machine. Not your stuff – the custard stuff.'

'Yes, but [I wanted to make sure this worked] if you don't leave right now, and I mean right now, the deal is off, and I'll just carry you out of here.'

'Are we getting one for Tadhg as well?'

'Yes.'

'OK, but I'm picking out the topping and [there was a pause] I'm allowed to get a juice as well.'

Christ, it was like I was negotiating the Iranian hostage crisis.

'Yes, but you have to leave now right now.'

She took my hand and we started to walk out of the shop. She had one more thing to say. As we passed Rock Boy, she shouted, 'Bye'.

He waved back, 'See you, Olivia, enjoy hiking with your dad.'

Of course, she stopped in front of him, turned to me and said, as loudly as possible, 'What's hiking, Dad?'

Eventually we got to the car. Tadhg saw she had an ice-cream and before he could protest, I gave him his. The two of them sat quietly in the back seat. I looked back at them and thought about what my mother used to say to us as kids years ago: 'You're only quiet when you are eating.' How true.

However, the quiet time allowed Lorna to interrogate me about my purchase.

'Are you going hiking?' she asked.

'Yeah.'

'With whom and where?'

'With Ronan, or on my own.'

'Bernard, if you go hiking on your own, you will either die or I'll have to come and collect you,' Lorna said.

'Sure,' I said. 'And why don't you bring Rock Boy with you?'

'Who?'

'I saw the way you talked to him. You know, he looked at you the same way he would look at his teachers or at an auntie.'

'What are you talking about?' Lorna looked incredulous.

'It was painfully obvious – you were flirting with him.'

'Yeah,' she said. 'I was flirting with him – with my two kids and husband with me.'

'It's alright,' I said. 'I don't mind.'

'Well maybe I should call back later and have a better chat with him, because I'll need to know how to rescue you when you go hiking.'

'Well, I'm going to hike anyway – you're welcome to come,' I said. I regretted saying that.

On the Sunday of the following week, I planned to go for my first hike. I rang Ronan and he sent me the details of an easy hike that I could do on my own. It was in Glendalough in Co. Wicklow, only 40 minutes from our house. The only hitch was that I had to go with my wife and two kids, who instead of bringing state-of-the-art hiking boots, brought a picnic. The plan was that they would have their picnic while I would do a ten-mile hike around the lake. They set up their blanket under a tree and I took off. My wife waved me off with great encouragement: 'Be careful, Bernard, don't do anything stupid.' The kids ran along shouting, 'Daddy's hike, Daddy's hike'.

I walked along the edge of the lake for about an hour, following Ronan's instructions. The boots felt tight, but I did notice, as I went further up the mountain, that more of *us* 'hikers' had a similar style of boot. Another hour went by quickly and I started to think that I should have brought a stick. I started to feel a tightness in my heels again from the boots, but I thought nothing much of it. Then I started an ascent into the woods, along a pathway that led into a small ravine from where you could get a spectacular view of the lake below. It's a popular walkway and it was quite busy. Again, I felt a cutting pain on the backs of my heels, but I kept going and made it to the top eventually. I was utterly exhausted and when I had the area to myself had a little cry. My neck was killing me. My knees were actually creaking. My ankles were in agony. The boots were slicing me apart. All I could hear was Rock Boy's voice in my ear: 'Break them in.'

I stopped on the way down and took the right boot off. It came off with a 'spluck' sound and a big pool of blood squelched out onto the brown-needled path. The boots had cut the ankles off me, but even so, I had no other choice but to plough on. I got to the path around the lake, which was about an hour's walk from Lorna and the kids. I kept going, with each step squishing and squelching blood around the boots. I kept going for another half an hour, but I had to stop. I was gone nearly three-and-a-half hours at this stage. I rang Lorna.

'Are you close by? The kids are getting bored,' she shouted into the phone before I got a chance to explain my predicament.

'Can you come and meet me and bring my runners from the car?' I said.

She panicked. 'What did you do?' I reassured her that all was well and half an hour later, I could see the kids running towards me, carrying a runner each.

When I took off the boots, Lorna could see what I'd done. 'You f**king idiot. You're supposed to break them in.'

On the drive home, Ronan called me. 'How did you get on?' I told him about reaching the top and about my bleeding heels. He said, 'You should really break them in first.' Then the hammer blow came. 'Apart from the boots, how did the legs feel?' he asked me.

'Well, I was utterly exhausted when I got to the top,' I replied.

Then he said, with no intention of insulting me: 'That's where we normally meet up to go on our hikes.' I'd nearly died getting there and that's where his club just starts out.

Later that evening, while we were all eating Rice Krispies, watching *Frozen* for the umpteenth time, Lorna said, 'The outdoors is not for you, Bernard.' But the whole episode was eloquently put to bed when Olivia turned to me and said, 'You should just do picnics, Daddy, you're good at them.'

I'll take that, because I am very, very good at picnics.

LIE NUMBER 3
'You lied about getting surgery so you could watch Netflix.'

I have lipomas. They are lumps of hard fat that grow just underneath the skin. I have them everywhere. They are harmless but not nice to look at and I've had one removed on my right arm for aesthetic purposes. You get a local anaesthetic and the doctor just makes an incision and cuts them out before stitching the skin.

I had one on the right side of my lower stomach that was beginning to give me grief, so I asked the doctor about it and she referred me to a surgeon to get it, and possibly more, removed. I went to see the surgeon and made a date with his secretary to have them removed two weeks later. As I was putting the date into my diary, I noticed that I was to be gigging that same night. Before I left, I asked the surgeon if I could work after the surgery and he said, 'Yes, no problem. As long as it's not vigorous work and you can't get the scars wet for four to five days.' So far, so good.

My surgery was due on the Friday and Lorna decided to go home to Limerick with the kids that weekend. She added, 'So you have no excuse not to rest on Friday night after they take your little lumps out.'

I corrected her. 'I'm getting surgery, Lorna,' and she reminded me, 'Plastic surgery, Bernard.' It's technically true. To get them removed in Ireland is deemed plastic surgery and non-essential. 'You're going to go ahead with this one, are you?' she added. What she meant by this was that it wasn't the first time that year that I had contemplated going under the knife for aesthetic reasons.

The previous winter I had filmed a TV show with my friend Marty Morrissey in New York. We took a lighthearted look into the world of men's beauty and one of the segments involved us visiting a plastic surgeon. His name was Dr David Shafer, a well-respected surgeon. He was a very amenable fellah and nothing like you'd think a rock star surgeon would be. He did a few fun items with us and told us what the most common procedures for men were. I thought it would be penis extensions. He did do them – in fact, he had his own method, called the SWAG Penis Enhancement Procedure, which stands for (no pun intended) Shafer Width and Girth. The same products that are injected into cheeks and lips can also be injected into the penile shaft and glans to increase penis girth and to moderately increase penis length. I've always been obsessed with my penis, and, guess what? So is every man on the planet. No matter how many *Cosmo* articles we read that say, 'size doesn't matter', we don't care. If a woman happens to say, 'size does matter', we collectively go, 'WE KNEW ALL ALONG'.

However, Dr Shafer told us that most men and women go for neck tucks. The operation involves making an incision behind the ear and pulling the skin back. He also put us on a state-of-the-art computer visualiser, which showed us the damage the sun and other pollutants do to the skin. For the programme's sake, I elected to get assessed for liposuction. Dr Shafer sat me up on the bench and got a green marker and started to draw on me, bringing me through what would happen. He marked out a circular area on my front, then two areas on my side and one on my lower back. I asked him how much the procedure would cost. He said, 'About thirty to thirty-five thousand dollars for the whole thing.'

I had never realised that it was so expensive, but even though it was for a TV show, I genuinely considered it. Never in a thousand years would I have thought about liposuction or tummy tucks or anything like it, but while the crew were setting up for the next shot, I asked him, 'How long would it take?'

He told me the surgery would take an hour for each segment, that he could get it done in two days, but I'd have to rest for three days before getting on an aeroplane. I jokingly asked him, 'Could you fit me in this week?'

When he replied, 'Yeah', I laughed it off, but then I snuck off into a corner to see what the logistics looked like. Lorna was expecting me home on the Friday of that week but, even resting for three days post-surgery, I could fly back on Wednesday and be home for Thursday. The cost was another issue. It was an awful amount of money, but I'd most definitely spent that on gyms, diet fads and, Christ, Tupperware for the nutritious meals I never prepared. Like most comics, I thought I could then do a show about it. It would be great material. But most of all, I thought that it was a genuine silver bullet. I could go back to Ireland in five days weighing twelve-and-a-half stone with no work, no sweat, no tears or guilt.

That night I rang home and told Lorna what I was planning. Her initial reaction was 'No f**king way', then she mellowed and said, 'If you think it would change your life, then do it, but I'm worried about you getting surgery in another country if anything happens.'

I slept on it. We got up the next morning early – very early. I looked at myself in the mirror in the lift as I headed down to breakfast. I wasn't massive – but I wasn't in shape either. I could have taken the thirty flights of stairs down and got a workout in instead of taking the lift, and that is my problem: I'm lazy. If I got the quick fix, would I be back to sixteen stone in a year, I wondered? Probably. I just needed to stop eating crap and take the stairs.

I made my decision. I'd give the surgery a miss. I texted Lorna. 'See you Saturday.'

She texted back: 'F**king EEJIT'.

Little did I know that, a year later, I'd be googling 'rapid weight loss'.

I regret not doing it. I regret not staying the extra few days and just getting it done, regardless of the money. My savings would have been gone but I would have been thin.

Now, a year later, I was going to get tiny little lumps of fat removed – not three stone in fat. I'm possibly the only person to under-compensate for a surgery.

Lorna headed down to Limerick that morning. We said our goodbyes: 'Good luck with your doctor's appointment,' she said.

'IT'S A SURGICAL PROCEDURE.'

When she'd left, I turned on Netflix and there in front of me, like some gift from the gods, lay the new series of *House of Cards*. I could now genuinely try, for the first time in six years, to binge-watch a complete series. I could then say with confidence to any Millennial: 'Hey, I've been binge-watching *House of Cards*.' I remember when you had to wait until the following week to see what was going to happen in your favourite programme on this thing called television. People would stay in on a Saturday night to see why Bobby Ewing took so long in the shower on *Dallas*, or if Crockett and Tubbs would foil a massive drug deal in *Miami Vice*. I once told my seventeen-year-old niece: 'If you think spoilers are annoying today, in my day, you could have actually lost a limb if you told someone what was going to happen on *Knots Landing* before they got home to watch it on TAPE.' Now, you can do it all in one evening.

It was 12:20 pm. That meant I could get three episodes in before my surgery at 4:30 that afternoon. It would take twenty minutes, so I'd be back around 5:30 and get one more in and then travel to my gig, which was about an hour-and-a-half's drive away. I would be back at 11:30 that night and I could watch another episode. Then, the next morning, I could get up and have breakfast on my own – yippee!!! – and watch the following three episodes before the family got back around midday. I got so excited, I even pulled down the blinds and turned off my phone. This was bliss.

But before my political-binge escapade began, I had to ring the hospital to confirm the appointment. When I was about to hang up, I asked, 'I'm OK to drive after it, yeah?'

The secretary said, 'Hold on, I'll ask the doctor.' She came back and said, 'You're down to get multiple incisions, so because of the seat belt and movement, you shouldn't drive immediately after. Also, you're getting a local anaesthetic, which can make you drowsy.'

I was in a quandary. 'I have to travel to do a gig tonight – I can't cancel.'

After talking to the doctor, I decided to defer the surgery. That's my story. I mean, that's what happened. Lorna's story would be more like this: Bernard saw that Season 6 of *House of Cards* was on Netflix. I was away with the kids that night and he was gigging. He decided he would watch the whole season. He would drive up to his gig and drive back so he could watch it all before we got back. Deferring the surgery was just a ruse. He is lazy and a liar.

LIE NUMBER 4

'You lied about being able to gut a fish and nearly went as far as to poison the children in the process.'

My father died on 8 June 2018. I'm so bad with dates that I had to ring my mother and ask her to confirm it. She didn't judge me. She, like my wife, knows that I'm not thoughtless, just innumerate. It was a nice role-reversal to ring her, as, like most mothers in Ireland, every time I call home, we play the Guess-Who's-Dead game. That's where she says, 'You'll never guess who's died.'

I play along by replying, 'No'.

Then, disappointingly, she reveals the answer. Ninety per cent of the time I don't know the person. Thus, Round Two starts, which is called You Do Know Them. She then gives a brief outline of their entire lives, adamant that I know who they are/were.

I reply, feeling the resurgence of my inner teenager, 'Oh, yeah.' However, today was slightly different as it was me asking the questions.

'Why do you want to know that?' she asked.

I didn't really want to tell her. I didn't want asking for the date to seem frivolous. But for brevity and honesty's sake I told her: 'It's about a dead fish Olivia caught that she keeps in our freezer.'

With three children under six years of age, family holidays for me are exhausting affairs. On some of our trips to the seaside, when all three of them have been screaming in the back of the car and they're only allowed to look out the closed windows for fear of losing one of them to gale-force winds, I often think that the Americans should have forced Osama

Bin Laden to build sandcastles on a wet, cold summer's day on Inch beach, while eating a 99, instead of killing him. Kerry seals, not Navy SEALs.

Now, with an added baby, it's difficult … really difficult. We had two children just out of nappies, walking and talking – as I said to Lorna (and she keeps reminding me of this) – 'We were just out of the woods and we went back in to start a fight with a hungry, angry baby bear.' So, it came as a great relief that she decided we would go away for three days in summer 2019 with just Olivia and Tadhg, leaving the baby with her parents, who were coming to Dublin to mind him. Even though Seán has a name, I still call him 'the baby' – I find it odd to call babies by their names. Olivia and Tadhg call him Seánie, but I still mostly refer to him as 'the baby'.

My father-in-law hooked up his caravan for us thirty miles away from our home in Dublin in a picturesque town called Roundwood in Co. Wicklow. Now, I have previous with caravans. I don't dislike them … I hate them. But the kids love them. They would choose a caravan over Disneyland any day, and all the donkey work was done, so it was a no-brainer.

We set off. Lorna was heartbroken to be away from her baby for the first time, but after about an hour a beautiful realisation kicked in: essentially, we were going on a holiday with two adults and two small people who were willing and excited to hit the open road … all within a thirty-mile radius of home. When we got to the caravan in Wicklow, the kids started to run around everywhere, exploring, risking life and limb. Another realisation hit: this wasn't a problem, because now, we could take one each. We began to relax.

The next day we planned to get lunch, then go on an adventure. 'Going on an adventure' means we haven't a clue what to do, but to the kids, it's an adventure. Their hopes were slightly dashed when I suggested we go for lunch. Even though Seán was at home, lunchtime with the kids is still around the 12:30 mark: early enough to avoid the work rush and single people but late enough for us all to be hungry. Olivia and Tadhg expect that every restaurant serves spaghetti bolognese. This is because my laziness has spread to their meals. I know good food habits form at an early age – that's why, from the very beginning, I would push them towards spaghetti bolognese as opposed to their other favourites, chicken and chips, or the house special that is 'I want your dinner, Daddy, I don't like this.' Plus, the restaurants near us are mostly Italian. I also order spaghetti online when I'm on my own with them. They actually get a kick when the delivery guy comes to the door, once described by Tadhg as 'the pasgeti man'. Tadhg now automatically thinks all delivery people are bringing him pasta. Trying to convince a hungry three-year-old that an Amazon package is not lunch isn't easy.

Now, we were sitting down at a local restaurant. The kids were not impressed when the waitress told them she did not have their favourite dish. 'How about sausage and chips or chicken and chips?' I said.

'Noooooooo, I want pasgeti bognase, Dadddddddy.' Fear rushed through me. Was the spell broken? Was the illusion that I'd conjured up the day before gone? Was this perfect little getaway to be destroyed by the lack of a regional Italian pasta dish?

Luckily, my wife stepped in. 'They will have the mini burgers,' she said decisively. If I'd said it, they would have just moaned, but when Mammy said it? Well, they might as well have thrown her a parade. Forty minutes and two mini burgers later, they'd also polished off their glasses of diluted orange. Just enough sugar to get them excited but not enough to give them a comedown.

We drove off on our 'adventure', passing over a little bridge, when we spotted a handmade signpost: Catch Your Own Fish Here. Excited, we pulled into a little lane and what presented itself was one of the most Irish tourist attractions ever. There was a little hut in a field with two teenagers in it, sitting behind a makeshift counter. Behind them was a picturesque river with a small sandy bank.

I asked one of the lads, 'Does everybody catch a fish? How does that happen?'

'It's a trout farm, they re-stock the river here.'

I didn't question it. For €10, you got a rod and some bait. They didn't accept cards, strangely enough, and directed me to an ATM in the village, so I jumped into the car while Lorna and the kids stood eagerly awaiting their first angling experience. As I drove to the shop, I remembered fishing when I was a kid. There was a river that had a decent supply of fish nearby. My friends fished all the time and I'd go with them. I must have fished for at least seven years and I never caught anything. In fact, it was a running joke that all I ever caught was a flu. Even as a young boy, I understood that I would have been a failure as a caveman because I couldn't hunt or fish. Still, I would daydream that I'd be in my little cave all on my own with no partner – a scenario I actually experienced a decade later, living in various bedsits in Dublin.

One memory from childhood stands out though. I remember getting a new fishing rod for my eighth birthday. I had begged my mother for it and told her I would catch loads of fish with it, as my current tools were inferior. Delighted with my new kit, I went to the river with my friends. A few hours later they were laden down with wild trout. I had nothing. As we were about to leave, one of my friend's sisters came down, bringing with her the news from civilisation that all our 'teas were ready'. She brought her younger sister, who was five, along with her. Making the excuse that there was something definitely wrong with my choice of bait, I started to pack up. The little girl asked me if she could have a turn on my new fishing rod. She cast out and within seconds she screamed, 'I think I have something!' Three minutes later, that five-year-old girl had caught a fish and also embedded a deep sense of failure solidly within my brain.

So, standing beside her, instead of having the foresight to just relinquish any thoughts of my abilities as a hunter, I decided to cast out one more time. I was determined to catch a fish and drew the rod back as far as I could, before lashing out the line. I suddenly felt an incredible pain in my head. As I threw the rod away, it got worse. I had caught my own head. I had hooked myself in the scalp. Badly. After four eight-year-old boys, a ten-year-old and a five-year-old girl gave it a full medical examination, it was agreed that I should go home for my tea. The hook was still in my scalp.

When I got home, my mother tried to get it out but couldn't. It was now really embedded into the scalp. My father thought it was hilarious, even though he'd been annoyed that I'd come home making noise while he was watching the news. When the news was on, nobody was allowed to move, let alone try to get a fishing hook out of their head.

My mother, for some reason, thought about bringing me to the vet.

'The vet? Why would you bring me to the vet? They look after animals,' I screamed. Maybe she thought she could get me de-wormed at the same time.

Looking back, I can see that she was probably apoplectic with the shock of seeing her son's self-inflicted injury, which would probably leave a lifelong scar on his head. After nearly an hour, which coincided with the news finishing, my father pulled it out with his pliers. Yes, pliers. My mother cleaned my wound and put a plaster on it. I had my tea and was told to get outside and 'Let the air get at it', so I stayed playing outside until it got dark. If that happened to any of my kids today, we'd be in the children's hospital demanding a CT scan and an MRI. In 1987, I guess the Irish medical system relied a lot more on families having a good set of pliers at home.

I was determined, now, to get an aquatic rewrite of my childhood. However, the queue at the ATM in the shop was at least eight people deep. I stumbled into some small talk with the person in front of me. She was also there to get money to go fishing, as was the person behind me. We eventually fathomed that everybody in the queue was going fishing. We collectively called ourselves the 'fishing line' – a terrible joke. Yet it succeeded in binding us together. As one person would leave the queue, somebody else would shout, 'Leave some for us,' or 'There's something fishy about that fella,' or my personal favourite: 'We'll have to scale this back'. (That was mine. No-one laughed.) Everybody in that queue looked exactly like me or Lorna – there was even a man my age wearing chinos that had been stamped with the official seals of three-year-olds – sticky fingerprints. Our eyes met. We looked at each other like two battle-hardened World War II soldiers. We knew we would somehow get through this.

When I eventually got back to the river, Olivia greeted me with her new saying, 'What took you so long, Mister?' She was beginning to go through a phase where she didn't see me as an amazing superhero; she now saw me more like how Lorna sees me: as a bit of a lazy person.

I turned to Lorna, 'She picks it up from you, you know.'

'Don't start, Bernard,' Lorna said. 'She saw it on *Barbie's Dream House.' Barbie's Dream House* was Olivia's new programme at the time. We would be travelling along in the car and out of nowhere she would say, 'Oh my gosh, just look at those gorgeous trees, aren't they just fabulous?'

Tadhg would constantly be irritated by these Cali-Girl outbursts. 'What are you talking about, Olivia, there are no trees. Mammy, why is Olivia talking like dat?' It was Beverly Hills meets Hill Sixteen nearly every twenty minutes.

Now, he was itching to go. 'Come on, Da.' We got our rods and started fishing. The kids were mad to cast, but fishing is difficult, so I helped them. Luckily, I didn't maim myself this time. It was a beautiful setting, but even though it's a lovely family activity, fishing isn't appealing to three-year-olds, not because everything is instant now, but because fishing is slow, even to mature adults. I imagine that even kids back in the 1920s thought, 'this is lame'.

'Daddy, why haven't we caught a fish yet?' Olivia droned about thirty seconds in.

'Because we have to wait.'

'OHHHHHHHH, IT'S TAKING FOREVER.'

We had only been there forty-five seconds at this point. Over the next half an hour or so, however, we saw others catch fish. It kept our hopes up, but it also re-kindled the fear in me. I began to think that I had passed on my poxy hunting genes. Lorna and Tadhg were having a similar experience; however, Tadhg then went on a rock-hunting expedition, so Lorna was left on her own. Eventually I felt a tug on our line. I knew what to do. I had dreamed of this day – the day I would rewrite all wrongs. I would catch this fish, gut it and eat it raw on the side of the riverbank, proclaiming my early-childhood psychological trauma dead.

I began to gently pull it in when Olivia yelled, 'DADDY, I'VE CAUGHT A FISH'. Oh, yeah, it was 'technically' Olivia's.

'Daddy, Daddy, let me pull it in.'

Now here's the thing. Do you let your child hold the rod and try to bring it in, knowing that it will probably get away, thus letting them learn a valuable lesson in life? Or possibly give them an amazing feeling, understanding what it's like to actually catch a piece of living nature? Or, third option, do you say, 'I'll do it, this-is-my-fish'? I so desperately wanted to go for the third option, but we held the rod together and I helped her bring it in. We pulled it out of the water, and it flapped its way onto the sandy bank. She was screaming with excitement, but she also showed a bit of trepidation, grabbing onto my leg. Then, the one thing I did not expect: she roared, 'KILL IT, DADDY, KILL IT'. It was not bellowed with a west-coast, American-Barbie drawl either but with a fiery Irish accent. 'KILL IT.'

I calmed her down and explained that we were not going to kill it but would take the hook out of its mouth and put it back in the river instead. At least, that's what we were going to do until we were informed that no fish were to be put back in the river. You kill it and take it. The two young boys in the booth would kill it with a quick knock to the head with a flat rock and then put it in a plastic bag for us.

Tadhg, surprising me, walked over with one of his rocks and said, 'Daddy, put it back in the river.'

Olivia interjected strongly: 'No, Tadhg, we have to kill it.'

I looked at her. 'Olivia, will you please stop saying that.'

She was still holding onto my leg. 'Daddy, please, it'll come after me.' Thank God, I thought. I was beginning to think she was taking pleasure in its demise. 'It will know I caught it then, please, Daddy,' she added. I understood. She was worried the fish might want a bit of revenge. I explained to both of them that the boys would kill it for us.

The boys duly killed the fish and put it in a bag for us. As we were leaving, Lorna began to look worried.

'What's wrong?' I said.

'It's Tadhg – he's not whinging that he didn't get one. I'm worried that we'll drive away from here and in about an hour, we'll have to come back.'

Before we'd even got into the car Olivia had our trout named Fishy O'Shea. She then exclaimed, 'Daddy, can we make fish fingers out of it for tea?'

Before becoming a comic, I worked in restaurants for years but had never gutted a fish. I remembered my granny doing it years before and recalled that it's a messy business.

Lorna asked me, 'Do you know how to gut it?'

I have no rational explanation as to why I just couldn't have told her, 'No', but maybe I wanted to make up for my pathetic lack of caveman skills and reassure my clan, on a deep, subconscious level, that I could look after them. 'Of course, I know how to gut a fish.' It had been put in the plastic bag fully intact, with no ice or refrigeration, and I knew it would go off if I didn't gut it soon. I thought, what the hell. 'Yeah, why not try when we get back to the caravan?'

The drive back was bizarrely subdued. Lorna whispered, 'Tadhg is going to kick off, I know he is.' I wasn't sure. He'd shown great compassion in wanting to put the fish back into the river.

Then, one of the oddest rows between the two of them began. Olivia, in her newly acquired Cali-Girl accent, declared, 'I have a pet fish. Oh my gosh, isn't that so amazing? I have a pet fish. Fishy O'Shea!'

'Do you still want to eat him?' Lorna asked her.

Olivia thought for a second. 'Eh, yeah, I think so.'

I didn't want a screaming, mentally disturbed child later on, so I told her, 'He can't really be your pet, Olivia, if you eat him.'

She was a bit disappointed but was surprisingly clear with her answer: 'OK, but I want a pet when I get older. When I'm seven.'

Lorna looked at me, laughing. 'Yeah, that's a great idea, Olivia.'

Then, from out of nowhere, Tadhg said, 'I have a pet.' To which, of course, Olivia had to say, 'No, you don't.'

Tadhg lost it. 'YES, I DO,' he yelled.

'Well … what is it?' Olivia demanded.

'My rock.' Unbeknownst to us, Tadhg had dragged a fairly large rock into the car with him.

'Rocks aren't pets, Tadhg. Tell him, Mammy,' Olivia wailed.

Lorna was struggling to hold back the tears of laughter. 'It can be his pet if he wants it to be, Olivia.'

Then there was an odd silence – one of those calm-before-the-shit-storm silences. Tadhg broke it by whispering, 'Olivia killed her pet'.

I couldn't help it. I burst out laughing. This poked the fire in Olivia, and she screamed, 'NO, I DIDN'T, TADHG, YOU ARE STUPID.'

'Yes, you did, Olivia, you killed Fishy O'Shea,' Tadhg insisted.

Olivia burst into tears. Lorna tried to salvage the situation. 'Tadhg, she didn't. Fishy isn't a pet.'

'But why has he a name, Mammy?'

Well, well, well. That's a very good question, I thought. How was Mammy going to answer this one? 'Bernard, are you just going to sit back and let them fight?' Lorna said.

I had an ace to play: 'I'm concentrating on the road.'

Olivia was now a wreck. 'I did not kill Fishy.'

Tadhg was not letting go. 'Yes, you did.'

Lorna tried again to salvage the situation. 'Fishy is not our pet, Tadhg.'

Tadhg, holding and rubbing his rock like a Persian cat, declared, 'I don't want to eat *him.*'

Distracted by trying to mentally figure out how to gut a fish, I threw my dusty hat into the conversation, 'Do you like fish fingers, Tadhg? Because that's what they are made of.'

Now Olivia had a card to play. 'You are not getting any fish fingers, Tadhg.'

Tadhg was now crying. 'I want fish fingers.'

I knew there was only one thing to say to calm the situation down: 'Let's go for ice-cream,' I suggested.

Silence descended once more. After half an hour's drive we eventually found a shop that sold Mr Whippy ice-cream. It proved to be an amnesiac in the whole 'you killed your pet' row and when we got back to the caravan, I had time to Google 'How to gut a fish'. However, the one time I actually needed the internet there was no signal. I tried walking around different parts of the park to see if I could get Wi-Fi, but nothing. Eventually after looking at the fish for half an hour, I figured out that I could cut down along its belly and just squeeze out the insides. The kids were playing outside, so I got a basin and headed into the caravan. Here's the thing nobody ever needs to tell you: gutting a fish is a very messy job. I've been totally brainwashed by cooking programs – I'm obsessed with them – but as far as I can remember, I've never seen a celebrity chef clean the guts out of fish.

The first thing I noticed when I cut into it was the smell. It was really strong. The second thing was that 'squeezing' the guts out wasn't going to work. The third thing was that it was disgusting. If you're not used to it, gutting a fish feels like you're operating on yourself. Guts really feel like guts. I couldn't get them out. Then I had a brainwave. I would cut the head off and maybe push the insides up from the bottom. I found an old, blunt knife and started to hack away. I was making no inroads at all. Then I looked around and found that the van was covered with fish entrails. It was everywhere. I give out to the kids for spilling Coco-Pops everywhere and here I was, effectively being an aquatic Sweeney Todd.

Before I had a chance to clean up, Olivia burst through the door. She looked around in horror. 'Daddy, what have you done?'

I tried explaining to her that fish had to be gutted before eating, but she was in tears now. 'I didn't tell you to do this, Daddy, I only told you to make fish fingers out of him.' I tried to explain once more, but I couldn't console her.

'We're going to have to put him back together again,' she stated with authority. So, there we were, picking up every little bit of him, before I laid him out on the clean table. He (or it could have been a she) looked reasonably OK. It wasn't your usual Lego or Playmobil, but it was a reassembly all the same. 'OK, Dad,' Olivia declared, 'He looks better now. Put him in the freezer.'

I wrapped him in Clingfilm and put him in the freezer. 'Do you still want fish fingers?'

'No,' she said angrily, 'We will go for chips and we can eat them beside the fridge.' Then she quietly asked me, 'Can we keep Fishy O'Shea? I don't want to eat him.' We decided we would keep him in the little freezer in the caravan fridge and transfer him home in an icebox.

That night, before we went to bed, Olivia got up for what we all presumed was a visit to the toilet. But she opened the fridge instead. 'No, Olivia,' I said. 'You have just eaten, you can't be hungry.'

'I'm not hungry,' she snapped back. 'I'm saying goodnight to Fishy.' She said her goodnights and bounced back into bed. That was not the end for Fishy. The next day, as we were heading home, Olivia said, 'Bring Fishy, Daddy, I want to show him to Granny and Grandad.' I knew it was odd, but I did what I was told and wrapped him up in a bag and off we went on the half-hour journey home. She burst in the door of our house and proudly said, 'I caught a fish'. She let me display it to Lorna's parents and Seán, who tried to bite Fishy's head off as he was going through the worst teething in the history of teething babies. We'd got him one of those plastic teething giraffes and I've never felt so sorry for a vulcanised safari animal.

'Are you going to eat him?' Grandad asked Olivia.

'Yeah, we were. Daddy was going to make fish fingers out of him, but he's going to be my pet now.' Later she whispered to me again: 'Daddy, I don't want to eat Fishy, put him in the freezer.' That night she said goodnight to Fishy again and for the next few nights until she eventually forgot all about him.

Months later, I caught Tadhg and Olivia rummaging through the freezer looking for ice pops. 'You said we could have one if we were good, Daddy you said,' Olivia whined.

'Yeah, Daddy, you said,' Tadhg piped up. When they collaborate in an argument, you know they really want whatever it is they've decided on.

Then Olivia screamed. She had discovered Fishy. 'It's Fishy! We forgot about him.'

I took him out of the freezer. Olivia was mesmerised. 'How long has he been in there?'

'A few months,' I replied. To a five-year-old that means nothing. 'How long is that, Daddy?' Olivia asked.

'Oh, it's a very long time.'

She was still totally captivated. 'So, he's been in there for ages and I can say hello to him again?'

'Yeah, you can.' She said hello and then casually added, 'You should have put Grandad O'Shea in there, Daddy, you could say hello to him every day then.' I smiled and said unfortunately our freezer wasn't big enough. I was completely floored. All the memories raced back into my brain. I was overcome with emotion. It's not quite the ending of a Disney movie – 'Let's put Grandad in the freezer' – but for that second, I wished I could say hello to him again.

Then Olivia grabbed my face in both her hands and said, 'Hey, Mister, what's taking you so long? Where's our ice pops?' I gave her two: one for her and one for Tadhg. I closed the fridge door and said goodbye. Goodbye one last time to Fishy O'Shea.

LIE NUMBER 5
'You lied about meeting Nelson Mandela.'

In 2007, I went to South Africa to do stand-up with other Irish comedians as part of a mini-Irish festival to promote the country. We stayed in a place called Sandtown in Johannesburg and were to perform in the cinema there. At the time, I was doing a piece about Jesus and the Last Supper. The idea was that on the night before he gets married, he meets the lads for a meal. Half-way through, a Roman stripper shows up, Judas gets drunk and kisses him. Then the rest of them tie him to a cross and leave him for dead with just his underpants on. He gets so wasted, he wakes up in a cave three days later. The only one waiting for him is his fiancée, Mary Magdalene. She is really pissed off and tells him unequivocally, 'Get on the donkey, we are going home.'

He protests saying, 'I think I'm the son of God.'

She replies, 'I think you are a prick.' It all culminates with Jesus asking Mary Magdalene if they can 'stop in Nazareth for a Lucozade'.

I had been doing the routine for about a year, to varying degrees of success. Ireland still has the remnants of staunch Catholicism, but I never received any criticism for its religious content – more for it possibly not being that hilarious. However, one thing I hadn't counted on was how seriously some South Africans would take it. After one performance, there was a meet-and-greet in the cinema foyer. There were a few photographers from local papers there and some of the Irish community living in Johannesburg. A big man approached me and shook my hand. 'Bernard, you are a funny man, but Jesus's name is sacred.'

I started laughing, thinking he was just slagging me. However, he continued, 'Why would you want to upset my family and our faith?'

I was now on high alert. This guy wasn't messing.

'I'm not,' I said. 'It's a comedy gig. It's only a joke, it's not intentionally hurtful.'

'Then why would you talk about the Lord Jesus Christ in such a terrible way?'

I replied that most people automatically know when coming to a comedy gig that there will be comedy.

He was now slightly on the back foot. He moved closer to me and said, 'Apologise.'

Instantly, I replied, 'No, it's a comedy gig. If you're insulted, don't come back.'

At this stage, my friend Neil saw what was going on and calmly said, 'Don't engage with him, come on.'

Then the man said, very loudly, 'If you do that joke again tomorrow night, I will get my shotgun and shoot you.' It was true. Most South Africans told me that he might well appear with a shotgun. In Ireland when someone threatens you that blatantly, we just don't take it all that seriously. I worked as a barman for years and when I had to cut off a drunk fella, he would normally threaten my life, so in a perverse way I got used to it. I dismissed the man's threats, and then a woman from the Irish Tourist Board strolled over and said, 'Can we have him for a few photographs first?' and dragged me away.

That night, at dinner, the other comedians continually took the piss out of me: 'Bernard, can you pass the salt because, if you don't, I'll get my shotgun and shoot you.' Then, 'Bernard, are you paying the bill? Because, if you don't …' After dinner I lay in my hotel bed and wondered if he were to come back to the gig tomorrow night, would he conceal his shotgun and smuggle it in? If he did, then he would have a clear shot at me on the stage. However, if he didn't, he would have to either go out to his car or go back home to get it and then he'd try to bring it back into the theatre, so it would give me a chance to get away. Then I thought, why would he go back to the same gig again to see the same material? Either way, I was genuinely shook by the ordeal but, knowing that the material worked, I wasn't changing it. That's the life of a stand-up: sometimes it's better to actually die rather than to die on stage. The next night I did the same gag. Luckily for me, I didn't get shot. Always a bonus.

The following day we were invited to a lunch in a very fancy hotel about an hour away from Johannesburg to meet Irish politicians and dignitaries, as well as Irish musicians. One of the big selling points of this hotel was that Nelson Mandela had stayed there for a time after being released from prison and wrote his autobiography, *Long Walk to Freedom*, there.

When I told Lorna the story about the South African threatening to shoot me, we were probably on our third or fourth date. She didn't seem that entertained or wowed by it. I reiterated to her, 'Yeah, he was going to kill me,' but still, she wasn't that bowled over.

I was just trying to impress her, so I slightly bent the truth. I told her that the next day we'd gone to a fancy hotel, the very place where Nelson Mandela had stayed and written his autobiography.

She immediately sat up, looking impressed, so, to gild the lily slightly, I said, 'I met him'.

'Who?'

'Mandela.'

'Oh my God, you met Nelson Mandela?' She was seriously impressed, but I tried to look casual about it.

'Yeah.'

'How?'

'I told you, he was a regular at the hotel.'

'Did you talk to him?' she asked me.

'Eh … well I said hello and he kind of nodded back,' I lied.

'That must have been amazing.'

'Yeah it was … cool.'

'And did Karl and Neil meet him as well?' she asked, referring to the two other Irish comedians on the trip.

Now here's the thing with lying – it's a pain in the arse if there are witnesses. And, if you tell one lie, you generally end up telling about seven more to cover the first one. But I was too committed now to back down. 'Yeah, they met him too.'

'That must've been amazing. That's one of those incredible, life-changing moments.'

'Yeah, it was,' I agreed. (Or it would have been, if I'd actually met him.) For years afterwards, any time we'd meet South Africans, Lorna would declare with great pride, 'Oh, my husband met Nelson Mandela.'

Once, on a holiday to Croatia, we were on an island cruise on a little boat. There was a South African couple beside us, and Lorna told them the story. However, unlike the other South Africans we'd met, we were stuck on a small boat in the Adriatic with them, so they kept asking questions:

'Was he in good health?'

'How did you get through security?'

'Why was he there?'

'Was Winnie with him?'

Eventually, the woman asked, 'Did you get a photograph with him?'

'No,' I said.

'Why not? That was the opportunity of a lifetime!' She sounded actually quite angry with me.

I had to improvise. 'It was really quick: nobody had a camera.'

Her partner began to smell the bullshit. 'Are you sure it was Mandela?'

My wife came riding in on her white horse of truth to save the day and my blushes. 'Yeah, it was Mandela, there were two other Irish comedians there too, and they met him.'

He looked at me and said, 'You are a comedian?'

Glad at the change of subject, I went on to tell them the story about the man threatening me after the gig, and both of them agreed that 'Yeah, some people take their religion very seriously at home.' The woman added baldly: 'A lot of people are shot for a lot less.'

Almost ten years later, I was gigging at a comedy festival in Dublin. My wife, who normally has no interest in watching me, was meeting friends there so she came along. After the gig, we were backstage and Lorna was talking to my friend Karl's partner, Rachel. I joined them and we started talking about holidays and holiday destinations. Rachel said, 'South Africa was amazing.'

'Oh, I've heard that,' Lorna said, 'Were you there with Karl and Neil years ago?' Lorna asked Rachel.

Rachel thought for a second before saying, 'Yes, I was. We went to Cape Town and Bernard and Neil went on safari.'

Lorna quizzed her: 'Did you meet Nelson Mandela with the lads as well?' Rachel started laughing. 'No, we didn't.'

I pulled Lorna away and told her the truth.

She was really annoyed with me. 'You made a fool out of me for years in front of people.'

'No, I didn't. Sure, they wouldn't know,' I argued.

'What about that couple in Croatia? My South African friend in work? They all think you met him.'

'Do you have a South African friend at work?'

She ignored this attempt at distraction. 'I can't believe a word that comes out of your mouth.'

'I only said it to impress you, because you weren't impressed that my life was threatened,' I explained.

'Ah, cop on,' Lorna snapped, 'Everybody has had someone tell them they'd kill them.'

'No, they haven't,' I protested.

She folded her arms and glared at me. 'Stop lying, Bernard, because someday it will get you into real trouble.' With that, she walked off to meet her friends and all I could think of was 'I must do that old material again.'

That evening, I was MC-ing the comedy gig. I asked the crowd, 'Anybody in from overseas?' There was the usual array of answers and then I heard one woman shout up, 'South Africa'. I retold the entire story, including the bit about me lying about meeting Nelson Mandela. From the stage, I asked her to tell me if she found the Last Supper material offensive.

'Not really,' she replied. She was less sure about the lie about Nelson Mandela, however, and the crowd went 'ohhh', almost like they were being directed in a 1930s slapstick movie. I asked her what bit she found offensive and she shouted up: 'You shouldn't have lied to your wife.' She got a round of applause and then when the applause died down, she added, 'If I were her, I would shoot you.' She got the biggest laugh of the night.

LIE NUMBER 6
'You lied about being able to speak German to a group of f##king Germans.'

This one I couldn't remember. So, I said it to her. 'I don't remember that.'

She reminded me with glee: 'It was the weekend you walked into the glass doors at the airport.' This is one lie I will defend, as it was technically more a social *faux pas* than a flat-out lie. To set the story straight, I need to go back to a time when I had a 32-inch waist and Dublin was full to the brim every weekend with stags and hens, mostly from the UK and Germany.

I worked in a restaurant for years that was invaded by hens on their night out every weekend. Regardless of age profile or where they were from there was a familiar pattern to every one of them. I observed that hen nights resemble today's weather warning indicators:

Green Zone

Everyone sits down in an orderly fashion at the table. They look at the menu and decide on food first. However, even at this early stage, a leader emerges. Unbeknownst to her at this early stage, she will become mother, father, brother, sister and psychologist to every person at that table by 2 am. I used to call her 'Queen Mamma'. Most of the questions that I would be asked at this stage were 'Are there onions in the goat's cheese starter?' Or 'Can I have two starters as my main course?' Once I'd have answered all the questions the bravest soul would shed the fallacy of politeness and say, 'Will we get a bottle of wine for the table?'

Every time I heard that, I would laugh inside. That 'bottle of wine for the table' would be the starter gun for someone ultimately ending up on a table. I can honestly say that I never went and opened one bottle – I always opened three, because by the time I got back to the table, someone else would say, 'I'm going to have wine, too.'

Yellow Zone

We'd be onto the main course now and by this stage, I would normally have opened twelve bottles of wine. That's a massive 1200 per cent increase on the original estimate of 'a bottle for the table'. It's at this stage that you'd see little groups forming. One woman would drag her chair to the other side of the table to be with her friend, while another would be perched on the corner, talking to a new acquaintance who knows someone they both hate.

Now, the waters would start to get choppy because someone would always say, 'I'm going to have a drink before the mains come … Excuse me, can I get a vodka and Diet Coke please?' What followed would be a drink order that most Roman generals wouldn't have gotten for the Emperor Caligula. This was the lighting of the blue touch paper that sent us into the orange zone.

Orange Zone

By the time I would have the main-course plates cleared, somebody would be singing 'Sweet Caroline'. Now the shackles were off. I'd be asked, 'Are you the stripper as well?' God bless them. If I'd stripped, even back in my twenties, the money they'd spent on alcohol would have been wasted: even I have to admit I have a body that could sober a sea shanty convention. The groups were much more defined now: three at one end of the table in deep conversation, two women on the table, singing at each other, five all gathered around one of their friends and the 'Queen Mamma' floating around, checking in on each group while perilously trying to order everybody's dessert.

Red Zone

The desserts would be eaten, and we'd be on the fifth round of drinks. Queen Mama would desperately be trying to hold the unstable union together. The five women who had surrounded the one woman would now be in congress telling her, 'He's a bastard,' and, 'You're so much better than him.' The bride would still be singing 'Sweet Caroline' and would have joined up with a bride from another hen party, swearing that they should have a double wedding. Meanwhile Queen Mamma could be heard telling the manager she 'doesn't like her tone' and wants a discount because the starters were 'disgusting'. Eventually when they did finish, they'd head out into the dusk to the vocal embers of Neil Diamond's classic song.

The only exception I found in my years of waiting and serving hen nights were Germans. They usually had very quiet meals, drank moderately and were either horrified or massively entertained by what was happening around them.

I have been to Germany a lot. Firstly, as a teenager playing Irish music with my father and then mostly to football matches and stags … lots of stags. As you hit your 40s, it's interesting to see how stag parties operate. When I was in my twenties, I only went to a handful of them, mostly of cousins or tagging along with a friend. I remember thinking, 'Why are these men drinking so fast?' Now, I know that you get so few opportunities to get drunk when you have kids that when one *bona-fide* invitation comes along, you take it with both drinking hands. Now, on the rare occasions that I'm invited to one, I either pass out before the meal is over or slip off to get a night's sleep.

On most stag nights, it's every man for himself. If you pass out on the street, that's your bed for the night. Now, I just dream about being drunk and imagine the fun I'd have falling asleep on a nightclub toilet. Now, every night is taken up with trying to put the kids to bed, which is almost like a stag do in a way. I bring one-and-a-half-year-old Seán to bed, while my wife takes Olivia and Tadhg. When they get a sense that 'Blanket Street' is looming, they get a massive surge of energy and suddenly want to play in the back garden. On a stag, this would be when you'd end up in a hellish nightclub clinging to your youth while pretending to like the awful music by nodding your head to the beat. You think you look cool, while everybody under twenty-seven thinks you are having a mild stroke.

However, the thing about stag dos that I've never liked – and I'll never have to lie to my wife about – is going to strip clubs. I think it's the Catholic in me. Even when I see them on telly, all I can think of is 'She's going to get a chest infection, and ringworm off that pole.' They are, to me, the cul de sacs of the night – you can turn around in them, but you know the night is over. Also, I'm always way too paranoid that somebody in there might see me and tell my mother (another Irish trait). By the time it would get back to her that 'Bernard was in a strip club', the news would be so rancidly infected by Chinese whispers that it would be 'Bernard is a drug dealer who owns a strip club and he's a front for the Mafia.'

Caring what others think about me is a trait that I find both funny and infuriating at the same time. When I hear people say, 'Oh, I don't care what anybody thinks of me,' my gut instinct is to think they absolutely do one-hundred-per-cent care what people think about them. It's completely natural, on a human level, to care. As I get older, I constantly hit little truth milestones and one of them is that I care what other people think of me. I want others to like me. I once read that this is a trait that's common in people with low self-confidence. However, I have plenty of confidence, possibly too much – it's just that I want people to think I'm kind and considerate and friendly without having to put in all the work.

It was that 'truth milestone', along with a healthy dose of paranoia, that forced me to lie about my ability to speak German. I did take German in school for two weeks in first year but dropped out. The only thing I learned was how to count to twenty and that I was terrible at languages. I've always felt I could speak foreign languages, mostly because of the Eurovision Song Contest. Ireland just couldn't stop winning the Eurovision in the 80s and 90s. We took it for granted and it's probably the only reason why I can count to twelve in French. I worked out that the only German I would ever need was 'Ein Bier, bitte' and 'Noch ein Bier, bitte', because most Germans have excellent English. However, when I was working in the restaurant with all the hen nights, I picked up a few phrases for the German groups:

'Guten Abend, meine Damen, ich nehme an, Sie sind in Ihrem Hennen-Abend. Ich will, dass du dich auf deinem besten Verhalten aufhältst.' This translated to 'Good evening, Ladies. I presume you're on your hen night and I want you to be on your best behaviour.' It would get a giggle and then I would go straight in talking English. It was, and still is, the only German I've ever learned.

Lorna and I decided early on in our relationship, BC (Before Children), that we would go on a weekend break to Berlin. She is always on high alert when we go to different countries. As I feel I have an ear for languages and that I can pick up words and meanings here and there, I want to talk to the locals, whereas her opinion is normally 'Bernard, if you even try to speak their language, I'm leaving you here on your own.' However, at this stage, we were early in our relationship. As Lorna would say: 'I used to believe you before I got to know you.'

When we landed back in Dublin after our break, we were waiting for a taxi. Dublin is a busy airport and it is a constant embarrassment to me that when tourists land, the first thing they look for is the terminal for the train to the city centre – then it has to be explained to them that the sign with the train is actually for a bus to the train station and that you would be quicker getting a bus or a taxi into town. On the flip side, most Irish people just naturally expect a rail system in every European airport they land in. I was once stuck in Bergamo airport in Italy and I overheard an Irish couple giving out that it was a disgrace that the train station 'was three miles away'. I thought to myself, that's normally the length of the taxi queue in Dublin Airport.

When Lorna and I were heading out to get a taxi, we were behind a group of German women. I heard one of them say the name of the restaurant I used to work at and I instinctively said, 'Guten Abend, meine Damen, ich nehme an, Sie sind in Ihrem Hennen-Abend. Ich will, dass du dich auf deinem besten Verhalten aufhältst.' They started laughing.

Lorna was very impressed. 'I didn't know you could speak German.'

I should have come clean and said it was the only German I knew and that I'd spoken because I'd overheard the name of the restaurant, but instead I said, 'Yeah, I speak fairly OK German.' To which she replied, 'Why didn't you speak any over the weekend?'

That was a very good point. Why didn't I speak any German while I was actually in Germany? 'Ah, I just didn't want to make you feel left out of conversations and I'm a bit rusty.'

Back then, she actually liked me, so she said, 'Well, they seemed to know what you said and it sounded great to me.'

Everything would have been fine, if one of the German women hadn't turned around and asked, 'Wie lange dauert es, amen Taxi zu bekommen?'

All I understood was the word 'taxi'. I panicked. Our flight was late, so I bet that they were late for the restaurant. So, I gambled. 'Oh, zwanzig Minuten.'

There was a pause. I thought I was going to be found out, but she smiled and said 'Danke'. The flood of relief I felt – it was like a reversal of the famous scene in *The Great Escape*, when Richard Attenborough and Gordon Jackson are caught out by the Germans while boarding a bus, when the German says, 'Good luck,' and Gordon replies, 'Thank you', thus giving the game away. There were only two couples in front of them and I counted that there were six of them, so they would need a people carrier for six, or two taxis. I started thinking ahead just in case. I would need to know what the German for 'two taxis' was. That was simple: 'zwei Taxi'. I was stuck on people carrier, though. I knew 'Volk' was 'people' from 'Volkswagen', but what was 'carrier' in German? If the worst came to the worst, I would just say 'sechs Wagen'. Then I started to think that that sounded like 'sex wagon'. I started to pray. 'Dear Jesus, don't make me say sex wagon out loud in a taxi queue in Dublin Airport.'

I would have got away with it until another one in the group asked, 'Ist es normalerweise so beschäftigt?' I knew she said 'normal' and the second-last word was 'so' something – I bet on 'busy' – but I hadn't a clue about the rest. So, I just went all-out and said, 'Ja', confidently. Again, it seemed to work.

I was fine until she replied, 'Ist es teuer?' My mind was racing now and faltering like an overworked Scalextric set on a Christmas morning. I knew she said, 'Is it something?' so I went with … 'Ja' … again.

And then my good-luck moment happened. The girl said, 'Können Sie per Kreditkarte bezahlen oder müssen Sie per Bargeld bezahlen?' I was to later to find out that this meant 'Can you pay by credit card or does it have to be cash?' To which I replied, 'Ja.'

The game was up. They knew I couldn't speak German. Lorna knew I couldn't speak German and everybody in the queue waiting for a taxi knew I couldn't speak German. Then the most embarrassing figurative dagger was plunged into my now-bright-red face. The German woman turned to Lorna and asked in perfect English, 'Can you pay by card or do they only take cash?' It's one thing telling a lie and being found out in a situation where you can leave, but we were all stuck in my big fat embarrassment trap for the next 45 minutes. I could see them constantly giggling to themselves and looking back at me. For the fifth or sixth time Lorna vanished to the toilet to avoid my shame.

My lie was two-fold: firstly, I wanted to impress a woman, but secondly, I genuinely wanted to please the group and wanted them to like me. As I've gotten older, I've stopped trying as hard to please others, but in the past, it's made more work and worry for me than was worth it. However, it's not the most excruciatingly embarrassing thing that has happened to me because I was just trying to make people like me.

In my early 20s, I was living in a bedsit in north-inner-city Dublin. It was a tiny little space, but it was central and because of that, lots of people stayed with me. One night around two in the morning I was walking down O'Connell Street after work, when I was stopped by two French girls who asked me for directions to their hotel. They made an odd-looking couple: one of them was tall, around six feet, with long blonde hair, and was wearing stilettos, and the other girl was about four-and-a-half feet with blue hair. Even though both of them were dressed in layers of clothes, they were shivering with the cold. 'Irlande is damp, non?' said the tall girl.

'Yeah and this is our summer,' I said. I looked at the address and it read: 'George Hotel, O'Connell Street'. They said they had been up and down the street for hours and couldn't find it. This is where I'm at my worst. Instead of just telling them, 'I don't know', I feel like I have to take on the role of ambassador for Ireland and, in this case, to make sure they got to their hotel. I knew O'Connell Street well but never heard of a George Hotel. I walked up and down the street with them for a least an hour and eventually they said, 'It's OK, thank you.' But I wouldn't let it drop. It was in the days of internet cafés, well before anybody had smartphones, and I knew one that was open late nearby. I led them to the café, sat down and 'asked Jeeves' (the forerunner to Google) where the George Hotel on O'Connell Street was. Several minutes later, when the page eventually loaded, it said 'Limerick'. I explained to the French girls that they'd booked a hotel in the wrong city. 'This hotel is in Limerick – it's about 150 miles from here.'

They panicked and started fighting in French with each other, but they eventually calmed down and told me that they were in the city to see a band in a venue on O'Connell Street the following night, before flying home.

'Are you going to see Wilco?' This was a band I was, and still am, obsessed with.

'Yes, you like Wilco?' the smaller girl asked.

'Like' was an understatement. 'Yeah, I'm going to it too,' I said, walking them up to the top of the street to show them the Ambassador Theatre, where Wilco would be playing. We struck up a bond with our mutual love of an alternative

Americana band and in a fit of enthusiasm I said to them, 'You can stay with me tonight and try to find a room for tomorrow night.'

They were overjoyed, but when they saw my digs, they started laughing. One of them actually said, 'What is this?' I tried to explain what a bedsit was, but they couldn't stop laughing. Then the tall blonde girl said, very seriously, 'We are a couple – we are not looking for anyone to join us.'

I went as red as a baboon's arse on a sunbed and started a Tourette's-driven monologue: 'Oh, I wasn't looking for anything like that ... I was only trying to help ... If I was in Paris and lost, I would love it if someone could do the same for me.' I was being honest. I had no interest in them sexually. I was just trying to be nice and wanted them to like me. So much so that I was offering them my bed for the night.

Then the little one said, 'Thank you so much. We are so tired – where will we leave the keys for you?' I realised that they thought this was some last-ditch hovel that I had spare, possibly where I kept intelligent trained dogs or my mistress.

I should have just been honest and said, 'This is where I live, and I'll be sleeping on the floor.' Instead I told them to leave the keys in my letter box and they could help themselves to whatever was in the fridge, knowing that I never kept anything in the fridge. As I stood at my own hall door, the tall one closed it in my face. I had been so desperate to please complete random strangers that I had ended up with nowhere to sleep.

I would have tried ringing friends, but I had no credit on my phone. As I left the building, I thought, 'What if they rob me?' Then I realised that the only thing I had in the bedsit was my telly and it was an old Philips tube one that I'd brought with me from home and that weighed a tonne. I was 22 years of age and quite literally fitted the Bob Dylan quote about having nothing to lose except for my bed.

I walked the streets until about eight the next morning before returning home. I put my hands hopefully into my letter box and thank God, my keys were there. I knocked on my own door and let myself in. They were gone and had cleaned up. They'd left a note: 'Thank you, Bernard, see you at Wilco.' I was delighted with the place. They'd really cleaned it. I fell into the bed and slept until 6:30 that evening. That night I met them at the venue. They thanked me again and the small one asked me, 'Can I ask you a personal question?'

'Sure.' I was intrigued.

'Why do you have that place?'

They still thought that it was an auxiliary part of my life, some quirky little habitat I kept as I would a pet. I looked at them and said, 'I stay there when I can't get a taxi home.' At the time, I was so broke, I couldn't afford a taxi to the end of the road. However, I felt like I'd invented Airbnb that night. I should be a billionaire today.

Skip forward ten years and I was still trying to make a group of tourists like me by lying, but German this time. That night, on the way home in the taxi, Lorna asked me, 'Can you speak any foreign languages?'

I told her the truth: 'Yeah, a few.'

Nothing's changed since. Just like the hen nights in the restaurant where I worked, my lying habits follow a very similar pattern to storm warning indicators. They start off in:

Green Zone

These are little lies like 'Yes, I've washed the kids' or, 'No, Tadhg didn't lose his glasses,' while I'm still looking around the room for them. A lot of these green zone lies are down to laziness. Like taking the bins out. It's my one job and I constantly forget to do it. So, when Lorna says, 'Did you forget to put out the bins again?' My 'lie-ply' (lie and reply) is normally 'They must have forgotten to collect it' or 'I left it out but there was a complication with the bill.' These household lies are the ones that wreck Lorna's head the most. If I was to put them into order they would be:

5: I put on the dishwasher again because it didn't clean the dishes. It's not because I don't want to empty it.

4: I can't paint the decking this weekend because it's going to rain (I've said this for six years).

3: I'm not hungover; I genuinely think I have food poisoning.

2: Yes, of course I did homework with the kids.

1: I'm sorry I'm late: The train got delayed/the traffic was bumper to bumper/my bike was stolen so I had to walk home.

Yellow Zone

The best example of a yellow zone lie is when it incorporates a green zone lie into it. For example, Lorna might say, 'Bernard, where were you?' when I get home late and she's going for dinner. 'I'm going to be late meeting the girls at the restaurant. Anytime I have to go anywhere, you're late on purpose.'

To which I might reply, 'I'm sorry. My bike was stolen. I left it locked up at the end of the park and it was nicked.' Lorna wouldn't believe me and would be pissed off and would leave to meet her friends for dinner. Half an hour later, I might get a call from Lorna. 'I'm here with one of the girls. She said her bike was stolen today as well from the end of the park. She reported it to the guards and they're calling her back now. What was the make and colour of your bike? I can tell them yours was stolen, too.'

So, I would have two options here. Option A: just tell the truth, or option B, say, 'It's a specialised black bike … oh, wait I just remembered I cycled it to the office I must have left it in there.' (Another lie.)

Orange Zone

My orange zone lies have a tendency to be of the official kind. They are lies that could have a massive impact on my life but luckily don't. You could call them 'un-calculated risks'. Lorna calls them lies.

The biggest orange lie I've ever told has to be when I was bidding on a house at auction. In fact, bidding on houses seems to be one great game of bluff. Lorna was seven months pregnant with our first child and we saw a house we really liked but didn't have enough money for. It was a 'closed bidding' system, which meant that you wrote down how much you would pay for the house and put it in a sealed envelope without knowing what the other people were offering. When I heard this, I asked the estate agent, 'But sure you could accept a bid from somebody who pays you off?' His reply was that it was all above board and witnessed. When I asked if I could be the witness, I was told no. So, I wrote down an amount that we didn't have, just above what I thought the house would go for.

When I told Lorna, she went ballistic. 'What if they accept the offer? We don't have that kind of money, Bernard.' Luckily, we didn't get the house and I didn't have to sell an organ either to put down a deposit. Lorna will always tell the truth to 'institutions' like healthcare providers and banks. I'm a little bit bolshie and think, 'Why does this large multinational company need to know if I have more than three drinks a week?' I gave up confessing to priests when I was fourteen – I'm not replacing them with a tired call-centre worker when I'm 40.

Red Zone

Red zone lies are the worst, because they are the lies you tell yourself. These are very powerful but fortunately only tend to impact on you. For example, I don't like or enjoy dancing but If I practice enough, I can just about get away with it. However, I have always told myself that I could sing. Over the years, I have had several novelty and comedy songs on the radio. I've sung in bands and with my acoustic guitar for years. And when I was asked by my agent if I could sing in a musical, I thought about it for a second and went, 'Yeah. No problem.'

So, I was offered the part of 'Grandpa Joe' in the musical of the film *Little Miss Sunshine*, which was coming to Dublin. Now, Grandpa is in his 70s and from Brooklyn. He was famously played by Alan Arkin in the film. On the other hand, I had just turned 40 and was from the middle of rural Ireland. It was the third time I'd been offered a part in a professional musical and I decided to accept, thinking, 'What's the worst that could happen?'

The worst that could happen did happen. I had two weeks to prepare, so I went to London to rehearse and it was then the reality hit. It's one thing to think you can sing with friends; however, it's a completely different ball game when you're a complete novice and you try it with trained professionals. After my first rehearsal with the cast, they looked genuinely shocked at my performance. However, the cast and crew were, as they say in the theatre, 'beautiful people' and with the aid of the musical director, I learned to sing as best as I could.

On the opening night in Dublin, I could say I was nervous, but I was actually close to shitting myself. My wife came to see me on the second night and gave me one of the greatest compliments I have ever received from her: 'I cannot believe you thought you could pull that off but I have to hand it to you … you got away with it.' It was an amazing experience and something I thought I'd never do. But it shook up my 40s for me. I knew I had improved gradually but as I stepped out onto that stage on opening night, I promised myself: 'I'm never lying about my abilities ever again.' Three weeks later I was asked about auditioning for a small role in a movie. My agent said, 'They are actually looking for someone who can ride a horse.'

'I can ride horses,' I said. Thank God I didn't get that part, as the closest I've ever gotten to a horse is sticking a pin in the paper on Grand National day.

With all this, it was no wonder my plans for my Weight, Body and Mind were failing. I had told myself a huge red zone lie – that I was ready and able to change.

PART FOUR

Still Looking for Answers

*O*ne year later, it was the day after my 41st birthday. I was driving home from the supermarket. It was during the COVID crisis and there was an eerie feeling everywhere. Nobody was talking. Nobody was looking at each other. It felt un-human. Our most basic instincts, to say hello or pick an item off the top shelf for someone, were now a health risk.

As I was driving home, I turned the radio on and heard a familiar voice talking about meditation. I'd worked with Dermot Whelan on a comedy show called *The Republic of Telly* for six years and now, here he was, on national radio talking to his co-host Dave about how meditation can help with anxiety during the lockdown. As I listened to him, my first reaction was to find it hilarious. I remembered him being a funny host of a comedy show, not a serious meditation expert. He spoke very passionately about the virtues of breathing and taking time out for yourself. It was the first time I'd heard anything about him being mindful and was half expecting a joke at the end of his speech. However, the more he spoke, the more I could hear that he had fully converted to what I saw as the cult of Mindfulness.

That night, I googled him. Its odd googling someone you know fairly well, and I was genuinely shocked to see that he had become a master of meditation. To give my reaction some context, it would be like your older brother, who'd once farted in your face and gave you wet willies, becoming a Tibetan monk. I eventually stumbled upon his website and for most of March and April, every now and then, I'd click on it, even though I never did anything more about it or even tried his suggested meditations. It just felt too weird. Still, after everything I'd been through the previous year, I knew that I had to change something. Eventually I rang him. We agreed that when the restrictions were lifted, we would meet up and he would teach me how to meditate.

I met him on a beautiful summer's day in central Dublin. After four months of lockdown, it was good to meet someone who didn't ask me for a snack or tell me that the telly was paused. He hadn't changed a bit since I'd worked with him. He was affable and had a weird knack of always calming me down. After a bit of chit-chat along the lines of, 'How are you coping with the most bizarre human event in the last sixty years?' he asked me, 'So, why do you want to learn about meditation?'

I didn't hold back. 'I would just love if I could calm my brain down. I have a hundred ideas constantly whizzing around my head. I get strong, sharp, destructive fits of anger that last for about thirty seconds. I want to be a calm person. I hate having a temper because people always say, "It's the red hair." I know it's not. And it's not just that I also have to do everything *right now* and end up completing nothing: I feel that if I was living hundreds of years ago and the Vikings were raiding our village, regardless of how many of them were coming over the hill I would kill all of them – but then none of the other villagers would talk to me afterwards because of how vicious I was even though I did it to protect them. I would be really annoyed with myself for not asking the Vikings if they would like a cup of tea first to talk about what they wanted. It's almost as if, for those thirty seconds, I become a different person.'

Dermot took a deep breath. I thought he was going to laugh. Instead, he said,

'Firstly, Bernard, not everyone is made to be super calm all the time. Some people have fiery personalities and that's okay. I do think you may have a negative view of yourself. You explode, then there's repercussions and it might seem like it's regular to you, but, in reality, it doesn't happen very often. It only lasts a minute. You don't stay in that mode all the time. You don't smoulder and carry it around all day like a lot of people do. Some people are like a bomb going off and whoever is in the vicinity gets shrapnel. You are like that. Meditation won't necessarily fix that, but it will help you to blow up less often and will help with how you feel afterwards. You will come back more quickly to a balanced self the next time. One reason for this explosive behaviour could be that you have a drive to use your talent to the best of your ability, but you make yourself productive to the point of hurting yourself and when you're exhausted, you lash out at others.'

It felt as if he'd been spying on my brain for the last few years. Everything he was talking about made sense. He went on:

'That same force, however, that same drive to succeed, can be used to help you. And, as I said, what is going to be more beneficial is the healing afterwards. The invisible judge is inside all of us and you most definitely judge yourself too harshly. Look, I know this might sound airy-fairy but there's real science behind it, because with meditation, you will be sending those parts of your brain that work on keeping you level-headed to the mental gym.'

I liked the sound of that. He went on to tell me about a 2012 Harvard study that was done with the University of Massachusetts and Massachusetts General Hospital. A research group got sixteen people who'd never meditated before to practise for half an hour a day for 56 days. At the end of the study, they found that this group had lower heart rates, lower blood pressure, fewer stress hormones, a stronger immune system and higher sex hormones. But what they also found was that there was a physical change to the structure of all their brains. As Dermot said,

'The amygdala is the part of the brain responsible for fight or flight, which you need because it stops us from putting our hands in an Alsatian's mouth and walking out in front of buses. But in the modern world, it goes off like a house alarm and never turns off, even when we're not in any real danger. The study found that that part of the brain actually got smaller in size and the hippocampus, which is responsible for memory, self-assessment and logical thinking, got bigger and stronger. Just like your body, you can exercise parts of your brain, shrink your amygdala and make your hippocampus bigger and that's really important because that's the part of the brain that we use for empathy. You will have kinder thoughts towards yourself and other people.'

I started telling him about my sojourn to Mass nearly a year previously. I'd been looking for something that I couldn't put my finger on. I was a bit shocked when he said,

'With Mass there are some similarities in terms of what meditation might be. For me, meditation is a form of Mindfulness. Mindfulness is anything that pulls you into the present moment and keeps you there. So, if you are playing the guitar, it's very hard to be regretful about something or worried about the future. You are in the present moment – that's Mindfulness. Meditation just pulls you into that space. The similarity with Mass is that you are actively taking time out for yourself. You think, OK, for these forty minutes, I'm going to do this for myself, for my own head. That's a positive thing to do because most of us don't even take five minutes for ourselves most days. If we do, we plonk down in front of the TV, but that's not taking active time out for your brain – it's just more distraction.'

Dermot went on to say that Mass was, essentially, you making a sacred space for yourself, that a lot of meditation is showing to yourself you deserve a few minutes to yourself – you're setting a boundary.

I thought about my experience with Mass and the memory I'd half-remembered.

'Yes,' I said, 'but they say, "We would now like you to take a moment to think of those who have passed." At first, I thought, why would you make me do that? You have just ruined my day. However, when I did start thinking of friends and family who have died, I found great comfort in it. It was the only bit I liked, but they never gave you enough time. I'd be half-way through a lovely memory and then the priest would say, "OK, enough of that now, let's move on".'

Dermot laughed and asked a question that I had asked myself but couldn't answer.

'Why do people go there? Because it's part of their day and if they don't go, they feel that something is wrong. It reminds us that there is something beyond ourselves; that there is something bigger than you that has your back. Meditation can place you in that situation. Mass is a gentle reminder that God has your back. You think, "It's not all up to me." I'm not responsible for everyone and everything I come into contact with today. There's a higher version of me. I don't have to micro-manage every single detail of my day.'

I started laughing. 'You know, I got really angry about that; when I decided to go back to Mass, I thought, "It's up to you now, God, to fix me".'

He started laughing too. 'You actually did the right thing, or at least were on the right path, because any exercise that allows you to slip into the passenger seat, even if it's just for ten minutes, is super. Almost like, "OK, I don't have to drive this thing". And that's what we are looking for. You're not turning yourself into a superhuman: it's just removing the clutter so that we can be ourselves. We don't need self-improvement; we just need to change our perspective on all the things that keep piling up in our way without us knowing. A lot of the time just being able to sit still is a massive problem.'

I could relate to that. Apparently, the University of Virginia conducted an experiment with adults, who could either sit alone in a room for fifteen minutes or give themselves an electric shock via a button that they would press. The results were startling: even though everyone had previously said that they would pay money to avoid being shocked with electricity, 67 per cent of the men and 25 per cent of the women chose to inflict it on themselves rather than just sit there quietly and think. One guy electrocuted himself 197 times.

I started to roar laughing: 'I WOULD BE THAT GUY.' But I eventually calmed down enough for him to continue.

He then started to take me through what he called a sixteen-second meditation that he'd learned from his teacher. I found it odd that it was only going to last sixteen seconds. When I thought about meditation, I had visions of me in the lotus position, drinking green juice, while saying 'ommmmmmmmmmmm', yet here I was in central Dublin about to meditate. It felt odd.

'OK,' Dermot said. 'Close your eyes and take a breath in for four seconds. Feel how the breath is going into your nose, down your throat and into your belly. Now, hold it for four seconds. Now breathe it out, following the sensation, for four seconds, and then hold it out for four seconds. How do you feel?'

Initially, I couldn't answer him. It honestly felt as if it was the first time in my life that I'd actually breathed. I felt, dare I say it, after 16 seconds … relaxed! I wanted to do it again. 'I feel really good,' I said. I had never considered that my belly could hold that much air or how quickly I was breathing before.

'Well done – you just meditated,' Dermot said.

'What?'

'It's not what people think. They have this perception of meditation that it's all hippies and incense. A simple breathing technique like that is meditation. Tomorrow I'm going to send you a link that I put together for beginners' meditation and I want you to try it. It's about ten minutes long. It's more breathing but I guarantee you'll feel fantastic after it.'

All the way home I kept breathing in, holding it and releasing it. I must have looked like I was giving birth. I felt relaxed, excited and embarrassed all at the same time. I never thought, regardless of how overweight or lazy I'd become, that I was forgetting to breathe. I was eager to try out my new technique at every opportunity to see how effective it would be.

I started to think of the last few times I'd felt angry at something. I instantly thought of the guy in the gym who constantly dries his testicles and body hair with the hair dryer. Then I thought of the man who told me I was using the leg-press wrong and wanted to show me how to do it correctly. And, just to complete my Holy Trinity of people who annoy me in the gym, there is the older gentleman who keeps breathing heavily, like a pregnant elk, in the sauna. I'd stopped going because I'd found them all to be so annoying. So, I just took a deep breath in, held it, and then released it. Instantly I felt calmer. My thoughts began to change. Maybe the guy who keeps telling other people about their 'form' and how they should use the equipment is miserable in his own job and wants to work in the fitness industry. Maybe the elderly man in the steam room who breathes out like he's about to leave this world is just exhausted and needs the warm air to give him comfort. And maybe the guy who dries his balls with the hairdryer just needs to be told gently to stop doing it, as it's disgusting.

Then I thought about the reason why I was driving my car into town. Over the last few years, my patience for using public transport has diminished to nearly zero. It's not that I don't find it quicker, it's just all the other people using it who make me want to do a primal scream with frustration. There are three main types of people:

Seat-Keeper People

These can be easily identified by the way they put their bags on the seat beside them, even when people are standing up because all the seats are taken. Now, some of them actually believe that their bag is a person but most of them are … SEAT KEEPERS. Once my wife asked me to keep her a seat on a train during rush hour. I didn't get on the train. Why? Firstly, to avoid being a 'seat keeper' and secondly, to avoid a row with her when I failed to find one.

Smelly-Eater People

I can understand that sometimes, people have to eat on public transport. However, there is always that one person who decides that an entire carriage would only love to smell their homemade egg salad at 7:45 in the morning. The people who nip in and out of the carriage for a quick cigarette between stops are probably doing so to ease their anxiety about someone else's smelly food. I'd take stale cigarette smoke over egg salad any day.

MY CONVERSATION IS REALLY IMPORTANT PEOPLE

These are the people who want everyone to overhear their phone call and are probably hated in the office. They are normally alpha males in suits two sizes too big or too small for them, subjecting everyone in the vicinity to their puerile chat, full of business jargon and overt status signalling.

'Well, I told them I didn't have time for the meeting, as Josh wanted me at HQ – ASAP. I also have big responsibility vis-a-vis the engagement with the stakeholders and with the market being volatile at the moment, I need to be all over that like a mofo. Also, I just can't get my assistant to book me a flight to Paris at five in the morning.'

Finally:

Cold-Giver People

Not alone are they happy to have a cold and to show the world how brave they are by travelling on public transport, they are also driven by the need to give it to everybody else. Before COVID, they would cough without covering their mouths and blow their noses like ancient Vikings calling troops to a raid with a longhorn.

Now I was trying to think a little bit differently about my fellow travellers. Maybe I'm afraid of people? Could I be a closet claustrophobe? Maybe there are things *I* do on trains that annoy people. I possibly need to be kinder to my fellow passengers. Or am I just so selfish that I have lost the ability to share my space with strangers? Do I have trust issues? Again, I took a deep breath for four seconds, held it for four, followed the breath out for four, and held it out for four. Aaaaah.

What else, I thought. What else can I breathe out of my system within sixteen seconds? Well, I feel constantly guilty about raising my voice at the kids, even though they do my head in, especially when we're trying to leave the house. They can never find their shoes. One of them is always screaming, 'Wait for me', even though we are still in the hallway, going nowhere. Getting them into the car raises my blood pressure and I feel this morning ritual has contributed to several parents experiencing burnout.

I concentrated on breathing. However, this took two goes. Eventually I realised that I'm the one who's really ready to go and I'm pushing my anxiety onto the kids. I needed to be more organised. I do envy kids though. They don't care about Mindfulness or breathing techniques. They will just scream and cry for absolutely no reason at all and 30 seconds later be completely fine. What's more, other kids around them take little or no notice of them before, during or after temper tantrums. They don't carry guilt around with them for the rest of the day either – just oversized schoolbags.

I started to think about how I'd get really annoyed because there was no air conditioning in Lorna's car. There are no buttons on my new phone either. Everything is touchscreen. I recently fell out with a parking meter in the city centre. Again, it had no buttons. What's wrong with buttons? Where have all the buttons gone? I spent at least fifteen minutes trying to buy a parking ticket. And then there's the lack of handles in public loos. Now, every public toilet comes with a series of buttons to press, worthy of a mid-afternoon US gameshow, before you can liberate yourself. The flush handle is gone due to health regulations, leaving people just looking at the toilet thinking, how do I flush this thing? I took my four seconds of breath in, held it for four seconds and let it out.

I felt calmer and new thoughts came seeping in gradually. Maybe I don't like touch screens because I like certainty? The feeling you get when you press a button is that you have actually done something to make the machine work. Maybe I like to reserve the right to call someone and say, 'I pressed the button and nothing happened,' instead of 'I don't know if the machine has accepted my money, it's asking what zone I'm in and my date of birth. I just want to park my fecking car and I'm late for the dentist.' Maybe I'm losing touch with technology and maybe I'm the one who's stuck and broken?

I took a further four seconds of breath in and released it. It didn't work as well this time as my middle-aged brain roared, 'And the fecking apps.' Apps give me unfathomable amounts of anger and frustration. Everything I buy needs an app now. Here is a list of things that I've bought in the last year that tell you to download 'an app'.

Smoke Alarm

Fair enough, the app for the smoke alarm is a great feature and will inform you if your house is on fire. However, in my case, it wouldn't work unless I hooked it up to the internet and permitted it to know my location because secretly it's a Russian spy.

A lamp

Why a lamp needs an app is still a mystery to me. 'Control the ambience of the room and on/off functions from the comfort of your phone,' it said on the box that it came in. However, can I not get off my seat and turn it on or off to control the ambience? I never knew that the ability to turn a lamp on or off was a 'function' but then again, I'm new to the whole concept of electric light.

A bathroom scales

I wanted to buy a bog-standard, red-needle, old-fashioned scales on which I could weigh myself. However, when I took it out of the box, I was greeted with the all-too-familiar 'Firstly, download the app'. Why? I just want to stand on them to see if I can be constantly disappointed by myself. Now, I have my fat percentages, water percentages, BMI score and a myriad of new ways to make myself feel depressed, but it can't tell me what weight I am in stones and pounds. It actually can speak. It tells me, 'You are a hundred and one kilograms' – it might as well be telling me, 'You were a Prussian aristocrat in a former life.' I just want to know my weight in imperial measurements.

A doorbell

We wanted to get one of those doorbells that show us when someone is at the door and let us speak to them remotely if we are not at home. When I set it up initially, it was brilliant. We never missed a package and could keep an eye on our house when we weren't there. That is, until the internet dropped, or your phone was on silent, when we'd miss the delivery. I actually got to the point where I missed getting those little slips in the letter box that informed me, 'You weren't here between the hours 9–5 on Monday to Friday, so you will have to find our depot in the middle of a very confusing industrial estate in the middle of nowhere, then navigate your way through the hellhole that is our temporary reception area and pick it up yourself, ya lazy prick.'

Food

Yes, even food now has an app. My daughter asked me to download the app for her ice lolly so she can play a game while eating it. The instructions on the most recent bag of potatoes I bought told me to 'download the app on how to cook these delicious potatoes to perfection'. But I'm not striving for perfection – I'm just looking to put them into boiling water and stick a fork in them to see if they are cooked. Why do bags of vegetables need apps? What next? Wait, there is no next. We have reached app zenith, app overkill, we have climbed the app mountain and realised that the only new worlds to conquer now are apps that support other apps.

Maybe I'm a grumpy old technophobe. Maybe I'm buying all those devices for control in my life. Maybe I just don't have enough patience to learn how to use them. But one thing is an absolute certainty. Potatoes don't need an app. I took another four seconds of breath in. I was fully conscious that there is a breathing app on my watch, but I went solo. The very thought of the app made me decide on a sixteen-second all-out war on everything that sparked my amygdala into fury mode:

* We never have small spoons in the house. Are the kids eating them? We have three food brushes and eight novelty vegetable peelers, but no small spoons – ever.

* Every single time I pick up a pen it somehow destroys a shirt or trousers.

* I can't open cans or bottles of fizzy drink anymore without half of it going everywhere.

* Every single time I have got to use an ATM, it's out of order. I'm beginning to think that a complex practical joke is being played on me.

* It drives me mental that when you ask for a bag in a shop, they just fling it at you. Surely it would be quicker to just help me pack it?

* Every PA announcement in an airport is a mush of mumbling and it annoys me that it can't be clearer.

* Nobody in the security queue in the airport is EVER READY, even though they've been told constantly to take out electronics, remove belts, etc.

* Why can't waiters and waitresses bring down the card machine with them when you get the bill and not separately? Why are two journeys necessary?

* Why is it that every single dog that I pet is shedding?

* Why is it that when I really, really, really need Google Maps it doesn't work, yet it will randomly tell me that it will take 33 minutes to get to work on a Saturday?

* Why do launderettes demand that you separate your colours before you drop off a bag of washing? That's the primary reason I'm paying a launderette: to wash my clothes because I don't want to do them.

* Why is it every time I go through a drive-through fast-food place, my order is always wrong and then I have to wait in the car park for it?

As I started to list the thousands of things that got me angry, then did the sixteen-second breathing, I realised the biggest issue. It was me. I find these things difficult, but I had become an instant convert to Dermot's tool for calming me down a bit. I was now itching to go further and really wanted to see how the longer meditation would affect me.

When I got home, it wasn't long before Tadhg and Olivia gave me the opportunity to try out my newfound magical breathing powers again. During Lockdown, Lorna had been taking the mornings to work and I would take the evenings. So, every day, at 6 pm, I would take them for a cycle. Now, we were about to head out, and I could see they were fighting with yogurt, literally smudging it into each other like a Jackson Pollock painting. I was about to fly off the handle when I took in a breath for four seconds, held it and then released. Afterwards, I decided on taking another approach: 'Clean up and I'll take you on a cycle.' Lo and behold, it worked. I thought to myself, Christ, how was I handling life prior to this?

The next day when Lorna came down at dinner time after work, I was excited to start my introduction to meditation. I told her, 'I'm starting my meditation course today, but already I'm finding a massive difference.'

'Bernard … I'm happy, but just do what Dermot told you, please.'

Now, normally I'd reply with 'What is that supposed to mean?' And Lorna would say something along the lines of 'You don't think you are a beginner at anything. You'll do one session and then think you're a professional meditator. You'll race into it and within a few weeks, you'll give up.' So, instead of the argument, I just did the sixteen-second meditation and replied, 'OK'. The world and my brain were alright with that.

Later, I lay down on the bed and opened the link Dermot had sent me. It felt so odd hearing a voice that you associated with comedy guide you through a meditation. 'Make yourself comfortable and warm. It's more likely that you will complete the meditation if you're warm and comfortable.' I paused my phone. I wasn't comfortable and this was my first time. I wanted it to be just perfect. I got more pillows. I fluffed up the duvet. I took the bold decision to even take off my shoes. I was taking meditation seriously. I lay back onto the bed.

'Now, close your eyes, then let's start by breathing in.' I couldn't keep my eyes closed, so I borrowed Lorna's eye mask. I lay down again.

'Now, take another deep breath in.' I took a deeper breath and noticed that my belt was sticking into me, so I took off my trousers and put them beside my shoes and got under the duvet. Dermot continued, 'Now, feel the breath as it travels into your throat . . .' I couldn't stop moving around. I eventually took off my shirt and put on the soft T-shirt that I sleep in.

'You have thousands of thoughts every day but each time we let our mind wander, we are going to redirect it back to our breath.' Then the door burst open. 'DADDY, TADHG WONT GIVE ME THE REMOTE FOR THE TELLY.' Olivia had decided to tell me and half of west Dublin her woes. She wasn't finished: 'MAMMY, DADDY'S IN BED.'

'I'm not in bed, Olivia, I'm trying to meditate.' Half an hour later, and after a mini UN Council meeting about choosing a programme on Netflix, I was back to my original position.

The guided meditation was very different to the sixteen-second technique. My mind kept wandering and each time I drew it back to the breath. Then I would start thinking about the time I was wasting doing this and all the work I could be doing. Then I started remembering Dermot talking about giving yourself ten minutes for yourself and the benefit of it. Again, I tried bringing my mind back to the breathing. I started thinking about how massive my belly had grown. Again, I brought my attention back to my breathing. Eventually I felt myself drifting into a weird space where I knew I was thinking about thousands of things but only saw a bright blue light in front of me. It was a bit scary. I kept thinking about my breathing and then nothing.

I woke to find Lorna hovering over me. 'You won't sleep tonight, Bernard.'

I was confused, very confused. 'What?' I replied.

'I said you won't sleep tonight. Can you come down? I need to take a meeting.' I looked at my phone. It was 6:30 in the evening. I had slept for five hours.

How had I slept for five hours? I got up and felt rested, but then again you would after a five-hour nap in the middle of the day. But here is the strangest thing. That night after putting Seán to bed at 9 pm, I fell asleep again and woke at 6:30 am. I remember Dermot saying, 'Sleep is the most important thing and none of us are getting enough of it.' I had a sleep hangover. I felt like I'd turned myself inside out.

That day at 1:30 pm, I lay on the bed and followed his guided meditation again. This time I slept for an hour. For four days in a row, I nodded off during the meditation, until the fifth day, when I felt rested but remembered the entire ten minutes. I constantly kept asking Lorna, 'Do you find me any different?'

'No, Bernard, you are still you,' she told me.

But I found a massive difference in myself. I still felt anxious and worried about random things but not as badly as I used to. I felt more rested and slept better at night. But the biggest difference was that I wasn't sweating the small stuff anymore. If the kids spilled a yogurt or flooded the sink with toilet paper, I'd normally fly off the handle. But now I just say, 'Clean it up please.' I didn't get angry if things or people were late or machines didn't work. I even started using forks to stir my tea, if I couldn't find a small spoon. On the days I didn't meditate, I found that I would slip back into my old ways, so I have to be disciplined and do it every day if I can. It's truly amazing how something as simple as sixteen seconds and a bit of breathing can change so much.

I now knew that I had a technique that could really help me to stay calm and focused, but there was still a major issue in my life to resolve: why I eat so much, especially sugary stuff and especially at night. My wife is an avid reader and I noticed she was studying a book every night called *The Burnout Solution* written by a psychotherapist and life coach called Siobhan Murray. 'She gives really good advice,' Lorna said, so, when she fell asleep, I decided to 'borrow' it. This is a divisive issue in our relationship. I often slag Lorna for not wanting to share her food, but that's because I steal it all the time, so she gets defensive. Not only that, I have broken or lost things that she's lent me. Take her hairdryer, now broken because I tried to fix it, even though it wasn't broken. I just thought it should be belting out more air.

Her waterproof backpack, which I borrowed but left in a hotel in France. Her keys, which numerous times, I have just outright lost, and the pièce de résistance: numerous phone chargers. I could compile an entire almanac of rows we have had over phone chargers and who owns them. Eventually it got so bad that she had to write her name on them – even on the cable.

Even so, I decided carefully to borrow her book that night and I ended up reading nearly all of it in one go. It resonated with me massively and the next day, I decided to contact the author, who runs a clinic. 'Do you think you can tell me why I'm overweight and can't stop eating ice-cream at night?' I asked her. We decided to meet up for a session to find out.

The day I decided to meet Siobhan was a double win for me. It was the day after restrictions were lifted in Ireland following COVID and to get into my car and just drive five kilometres away from home felt like an odyssey. Also, because I am stuck permanently in the zone of miles and feet, working out the distance restrictions took up an enormous amount of time on the converter app on my phone.

As I sat into the car, I calculated that it was eleven miles to Siobhan's office. I looked at the screen on my phone and something caught my eye. The run app was still on my homepage, along with the calorie counter. I had not used them since the last time I'd tried seriously to tackle my weight. It felt unusual that I was going to a psychotherapist and not, say, a plastic surgeon to 'fix' my weight issue, but I felt that the meditation sessions were cleaning out a lot of junk out of my head. As I drove to Siobhan's, I realised how the little things, like a drive and watching people go about their business, could feel so nice – just that simple little freedom of movement.

Siobhan met me with a smile and we virtually shook hands. She led me to her office, which was bright and airy with no sign of a therapist's couch. A little bit of me had wanted to have the classic Freudian experience that you see in the movies, lying down on the couch crying 'nobody loves me'. But thankfully it didn't feel like that at all. She asked me to tell her why I wanted to lose the weight and what had I done about it up until this point. I told her about nearly getting liposuction and eating clay and wearing a weighted vest. I told her about my feeble attempt to try and get fit again and my calorie calculations to track my weight loss by certain dates.

She listened to me for almost half an hour. She didn't seem at all shocked or put out by what was coming out of my mouth and responded very calmly: 'The fast fix – the liposuction – is a fairly intrusive procedure to get to an end result, but it does not address why you got there in the first place. It might be a blessing in disguise that you didn't go under the scalpel because maybe we need to look at it from the inside out rather than outside in. Can I ask why is weight an issue for you?'

As obvious as it seemed, I had never really been asked this question before. My answer was basic and honest: 'I don't like how I look. I don't like how I see myself or when I'm on telly, I think, "Oh Jesus, I didn't realise how big I am." Secondly, I know it's not me. I'm not saying overweight Bernard is a bad person, but I know it's not me. I was always the skinny kid. I was that football player that was told to put on a few pounds. I was always that rake-thin person up to my mid-twenties and I put on a massive amount of weight. Since then, it has always fluctuated, but as I get older, health-wise I feel like I'm struggling to carry it around. It's almost as if I'm carrying one of the kids.'

Then she insightfully remarked, 'It's almost as if you are carrying the weighted vest but you don't get the opportunity to take it off.'

I started laughing. 'Yeah, and I'm eating, sometimes at night, especially tubs of ice-cream, knowing that I don't need or want this. But in a bizarre way, I don't see it as a reflection of me being "unhappy".'

She took a breath in and said, 'That's interesting that being overweight and not liking the way you look – equating that with being unhappy. Can I just ask you to go back to your mid-twenties? Where were you at that point? Were you working?'

'I never really had a job,' I replied. 'To be honest, I don't really know where I was and what was I doing in my mid-twenties. I came out of college at twenty-two, then I went to do a masters and didn't finish it. I know the year when I was 23, I dislocated my kneecap trying to play football and it was a big thing for me at the time. It was crippling. I was living in a tiny bedsit and I was drinking a lot and I found that when I came out of college, I was completely lost. College is great because it's a great life and you know exactly where you are going and there's an end goal. I found the transition between college and the real world very difficult. I found going back into exercise after my knee dislocation very difficult – it was slower and painful. And over the years, I kept dislocating it.'

'So, you were going project to project, to the point where you were thinking, "I have no idea where the next cheque is coming from." How long before you felt OK about what you were doing?'

I had to think about it for a minute. 'I suppose it was around 2006. I decided to stop drinking and get serious about the comedy. About three months later I got a gig writing sketches for Today FM with my friend John and from then, for the first time ever, I had money coming in.'

'OK, and when do you think that this weight that you are uncomfortable with started to creep up?' Siobhan asked.

'I would say when I was about twenty-four or twenty-five.'

She then revealed why she'd asked me about how I worked. 'One of the biggest reasons for weight gain is stress, but not obvious stress. Not tangible stress, like being in a car accident or the breakdown of a relationship, but low-grade stress that does not let go. And when you're self-employed, it's really stressful because you are constantly thinking, What's the next gig? Add that continual low-grade stress to the stress of parenting and lack of sleep and you are left with a perfect storm.'

Then she added – as if I needed to hear it – 'So, putting on the weighted vest, eating clay and drinking gallons of water a day is not sustainable in day-to-day living. You are adding stress, because you're saying, "Can I do this every day?" What happens if I don't do this every day?" Then you are into a downward spiral of "Has it worked yet?" So, there is no consistency in it.'

Just like with Dermot, it was as if Siobhan had been following me around for the last couple of years. Everything she said made sense. I had a flashback to the day I'd moved out of my last student house. Then I paused and without consciously thinking about it said, 'I'm sick of having to have plans.'

'Plans are great, Bernard!' she quipped. She added, 'Being organised is great, but it is one of the biggest contributors to stress. I think what you need to be able to do is have a plan but understand that the plan can change at any given time. Tell me, is it for your impression of yourself or other people that you want to lose weight?'

Again, I took a least half a minute to think about the question, not because there was a right or wrong answer, but I wanted to give the one true to me. 'I don't like looking at myself because I just think that's not me. I'm not the person who eats a pint of ice-cream at night. There are times when I think, "I don't have enough time to do anything – but did I just eat that because I was bored?"'

Siobhan agreed. 'Sometimes we eat, drink or smoke mindlessly. When we are trying to figure out something in our heads or trying to be creative, like you, the mindless art of eating allows us to take a break away from our brain, so we don't have to think about stuff. We momentarily focus on the ice-cream. But if I ask you ten minutes later what flavour it was, or how it actually tasted, it's gone because it's not about the enjoyment of it. It's the exact same as someone who decompresses with a glass of wine or cigarette.'

I was beginning to understand. Just like Dermot, Siobhan explained that the anxiety and fear we feel are to keep us from danger, but we have forgotten how to deal with them. So, we use other coping mechanisms. 'Food is the anomaly,' she added, 'because we need food. You don't need alcohol or recreational drugs. And plus, after a long day with kids, you are exhausted. You give them the best food you can possibly give them, like fruit and vegetables, but when they eventually fall asleep, the reason you don't treat yourself the same way is that you're burnt out and need a pick-me-up, so you reach for the ice-cream.'

This was remarkably true for me. The kids often ask me for a selection of fruit on a plate for breakfast. My wife jokes that they act as if they are in a five-star health resort. I cook them dinners at home with vegetables and organic meat and they get hot meals too in the crèche. For snacks, they get chocolate sometimes (maybe too often) but they continually graze on bananas, mandarins and berries. Yet all I do is try and put the quickest, most scary thing into my mouth for nourishment.

We went on to talk about why my attempts constantly fail. 'I want you to think about the concept of will power and *why* power. Will power is going to get you three days of eating clay, wearing a weighted vest, and it will be short lived. *Why* power, regardless of what it is, will become your way of life. This is not about telling yourself, "In a year's time I will have lost two stone and run 10k." Who cares? It has to come back to why?'

She set me some homework then. I had to write five reasons why I wanted to lose weight. 'The idea of it is that you are drilling right down to the reason. You say it's not comfort eating, but if you look back to when you lived at home, the comfort of knowing that your dinner was going to be on the table for you when you came home. It was routine, it was solid, and you were not stressing about it. It was a given.'

I'd never thought about it that way. Even now, when my kids say, 'Dad, where's the dinner, we're starving', I love hearing it.

We took a quick five-minute break and I looked over my notes. In large capitals I had written down 'BREAK FROM YOURSELF'. The first thing I said to Siobhan when we restarted the session was 'It's interesting what you are saying about getting a break from yourself. I don't really drink much anymore but I love getting drunk because I feel like I'm getting a break from myself.'

'But if someone said to you, "Bernard, you can never have a drink again", would you be devastated?'

'No, not at all.'

'But if you could never have a dessert ever again, or ice-cream?'

'I couldn't live,' I said.

And there it was. I knew, deep down, that my eating habits had gone beyond my control. I realised that once I hit my late thirties and the kids came along, I'd stopped drinking, but I'd started eating. Siobhan told me that this hadn't happened overnight, so it wouldn't go away overnight. Previously, I would have been disappointed by this, but instead, I now realised it to be true. It wasn't about managing everyone else – it was about managing myself.

The biggest lifestyle changes involve understanding why you are doing what you are doing. Then it becomes easier to have that conversation with yourself, to say, 'Why would I continue doing this to myself?'

I left the session feeling as if a massive fire had been extinguished in my head. It wasn't an excuse, but the pressure of always having to have plans was causing me massive stress. That night, when all the kids were asleep, for the first time in months, I took a breath and asked myself, 'Am I hungry?' The answer was no. But what did I do then? Normally, I'd work away on projects while scoffing sweets or get a takeaway, but now I had another tool given to me by Siobhan. I had an insight that my mind had been overstretched, so I meditated for ten minutes. Then I decided, I'm embarrassed to say for the first time in years, to read instead of watching telly. I looked at our bookshelves and they were full of books that I had started but never finished – like most of my plans. *Ulysses, Don Quixote, War and Peace* – all typical examples of my over-reaching plan to read the classics. I took down a copy of *A Confederacy of Dunces* by John Kennedy Toole. When I say 'a copy', I mean one of four copies of the novel that I own but had never read.

I opened it up and inside was a note, written by a close friend of mine: 'This is one book you have to finish, you lazy prick.' I started to read it and nearly four hours later I couldn't keep my eyes open. I went to bed exhausted. But for the first time in over five years, I didn't wake up until morning.

The next day, I didn't feel the same rush of 'Oh my god my life has changed.' I didn't feel particularly calm or manic either. I just felt … OK. I knew I was beginning to turn a corner. But in the back of my head I knew there was homework from Siobhan's sessions, so when I got an hour to myself, I went upstairs and wrote out, 'Why do I want to lose weight?' Then I wrote down numbers 1 to 5. I had numbers 1 to 3 filled in very quickly:

  1: I want to look and feel better.
  2: I want to stay healthier for the kids.
  3: I'm vain and want to look good.

But I was stumbling on 4 and 5. I was trying to come up with answers, not really getting to the root of it. I knew I had a constant stream of anxiety and I also knew now that the sugar helped me to get off the hamster wheel that is my brain for a few hours every night. Almost worryingly, I wrote down:

  4: Because it's not good FOR ME and if I keep doing this, my kids will copy my behaviour too.

  Very quickly I wrote down number 5: What I am doing now is not sustainable.

Numbers 4 and 5 came as a shock to me. I'd never thought properly about why I wanted to lose the weight. It dawned on me that my appearance and the fat weren't the real problem. The stuff I was shoving down my throat wasn't the problem; it was the stuff I was cramming into my thoughts.

When I had my second session with Siobhan during the COVID outbreak, this time on a Zoom call, she asked me what the main thing was that I'd got from our previous session. I knew that the stress of my job and my anxiety had made me reach for a Loop the Loop at night – I might as well have been reaching for a brandy. I might not be hungover anymore, but I was putting on weight instead.

We then had a look at the homework she'd set me. I told her that I found I could easily think of three reasons why I want to lose weight, but they mean completely nothing over time. When I first started, it was how I looked. Vanity. Then it became unimportant on the list. Now, I know if I keep eating like this, my kids will end up eating like this. I never would have thought like that in a thousand years and it scared the life out me. That would be my biggest why now.

Lorna always says to me, 'But you can cook'. I've lost that joy of cooking and baking from scratch. My six-year-old said to me recently, 'Daddy, can we have some apple pie?' I told her that in Ireland we normally say 'apple tart', whereupon she asked me, 'Can you make one?' When I said of course I could, she replied that she'd never seen me make one. I realised that I had lost my connection with food too.

Siobhan was smiling and again brought it back to my main thought about being under pressure all the time and being unable to sit and be present for a meal because my mind was always working two projects ahead.

Ever since the Wellness industry infiltrated my social media, I've always disliked the term 'present'. But now I understood it. What's more, I felt I would have loved to go back in time and be 'present' for more things – birthday parties, holidays and even work itself. Just to go back and breathe in and think: 'This, right here, right now, is great', without having that little rat scraping my brain screaming, 'Next!'

The other word that has continued to piss me off for the last few years is 'happy'. Siobhan tackled it with me. 'What makes you happy? What if I said to you, Bernard, here's two million euro so you don't have to work anymore? Would that make you happy? I don't think it would. I think there is a hole that you are constantly trying to fill, and you fill it with project after project after project.' Not to mention filling it with food, I thought.

We went onto to talk about happiness in work, too. It's a bizarre topic for me. I've never really spoken even to other comedians about doing stand-up and what it means to me or them. Siobhan pointed out to me that most employees would prefer a verbal thank you instead of a Christmas bonus, because the validation is not there with a bonus. It led me on to thinking about why I'm not doing stand-up as much as I used to. Again, Siobhan had insights. 'Whether it is a small gig down the country, or a stadium, the connection you felt with an audience means that now, some validation is probably missing. You can do all the TV and radio you want but you seem happy when you are making that connection. You get a kick out of stand-up and maybe you need to start honouring that a little bit.'

It's so true – I never felt like eating a tub of ice-cream after a good gig. I've never been into hardcore drugs, but I'd bet my house that they can't touch the feeling that an entire room of laughing people gives you. And unlike food, drink, or alcohol there's no guilt or hangover afterwards.

In a moment of clarity, I said. 'God, I'm replacing things I really enjoy doing with food.'

She nodded. 'Helping you with your food issues could be something as simple as the joy of rediscovery. Don't go off and try to learn Italian or weightlifting but focus on what made you happy. What were the things you used to do that made you feel good? Start there, Bernard.'

What Came Next

I learned more and felt a million times better in those two weeks with Siobhan and Dermot than I had in the previous twelve months. I started to read and meditate at night instead of binge eating. Now and then I would succumb to a half-tub of Ben and Jerry's but at least I knew why I was eating it. I eventually made the apple tart or 'apple pie' for Olivia. It was disgusting and I had to throw it out, but I did it. I read all of *The Confederacy of Dunces* and took walks without a full bladder and a weighted vest. I even started playing the guitar again, just for fun.

I kept thinking about a Buddhist saying that I'd seen hanging on a waiting-room wall that said: 'To know is only until it's done.' What I got from that is that experience is the only way to learn, even if you nearly wet yourself in a shop in the city centre. Just understanding why I make so many plans and what the outcome of that is for me has been really important. I haven't weighed myself in months. I don't think I've lost weight either, but what I do know is that I'm happier and I can somewhat understand words like 'happiness', 'present' and 'Mindfulness' now.

We are just living memories. Walking holograms of people who have gone before us. We're destined to make to make the same mundane or murderous mistakes. My father thought the same way as me. Felt the same fear as me. As deep and as meaningful as I feel my thoughts are, thousands of men before me have seen their hairlines recede and chests become breasts. They have thought the same and done the same silly things in the hope that people would see them as lion-tamers, not discarded chunks of grey meat slung out onto the Serengeti of middle age.

I suppose that's why there is golf, a game designed to propel a tiny ball towards a hole, while giving you the illusion that your best days are yet to come. It's rare that you hear of anyone being mauled to death by a hungry lioness on the 18th green. I bet that if I picked up golf, though, I could become a professional.

Now there's a plan!